Blackbeard

For my Mum, Liz

Pirate Schooner. Watercolour, by Lt. Edward Bamfylde Eagles, *c.*1805

THE REAL PIRATE OF THE CARIBBEAN

DAN PARRY

THUNDER'S MOUTH PRESS
NEW YORK

Acknowledgements

Many groups and individuals gave both this book, and the television film it accompanies, much generous and patient assistance. The *Queen Anne's Revenge* Shipwreck Project continually provided valuable expert advice, for which I wish to thank Mark Wilde-Ramsing, Jacques Ducoin, Dr John de Bry and particularly David Moore, Curator of Nautical Archeology at the North Carolina Maritime Museum. I also wish to acknowledge my debt to Professor Marcus Rediker, who offered significant insights into the ways of seamen generally and pirates particularly. Dr David Cordingly's detailed guidance on the broad subject of piracy was of enormous value, as was Dr David J Starkey's help on the economics of the period and Dr Lindley Butler's advice on the history of piracy in the Carolinas. I'd like to thank Mr Mick Crumplin of the Royal College of Surgeons for his memorable display of pictures and instruments associated with eighteenth century surgery, and I'm also grateful to Amanda Graham for her kind work in the Bahamas.

Everyone at the *Cutty Sark*, Peter Goodwin and the team at the *Victory*, Professor Richard Harding, Nick Hall of the Royal Armouries and Iain MacKenzie and his colleagues at the Admiralty Library were all especially helpful over a period of many months. The National Maritime Museum remains one of the world's leading resources on maritime history, and of course this book owes much to its experts, particularly Gloria Clifton, Douglas Hamilton, Brian Lavery, Pieter van der Merwe and Liza Verity. I'd also like to thank the NMM's Head of Publishing Rachel Giles, and all her team, for their dedicated commitment and support. And as always it's been a privilege to be part of Richard Dale's piratical crew at Dangerous Films. Above all I'd like to thank my wife, Saira, who, having lived alongside a book on Blackbeard over the last eighteen months, may have felt that she'd been kidnapped and dragged off to sea as much as any of the people who appear in its pages.

Contents

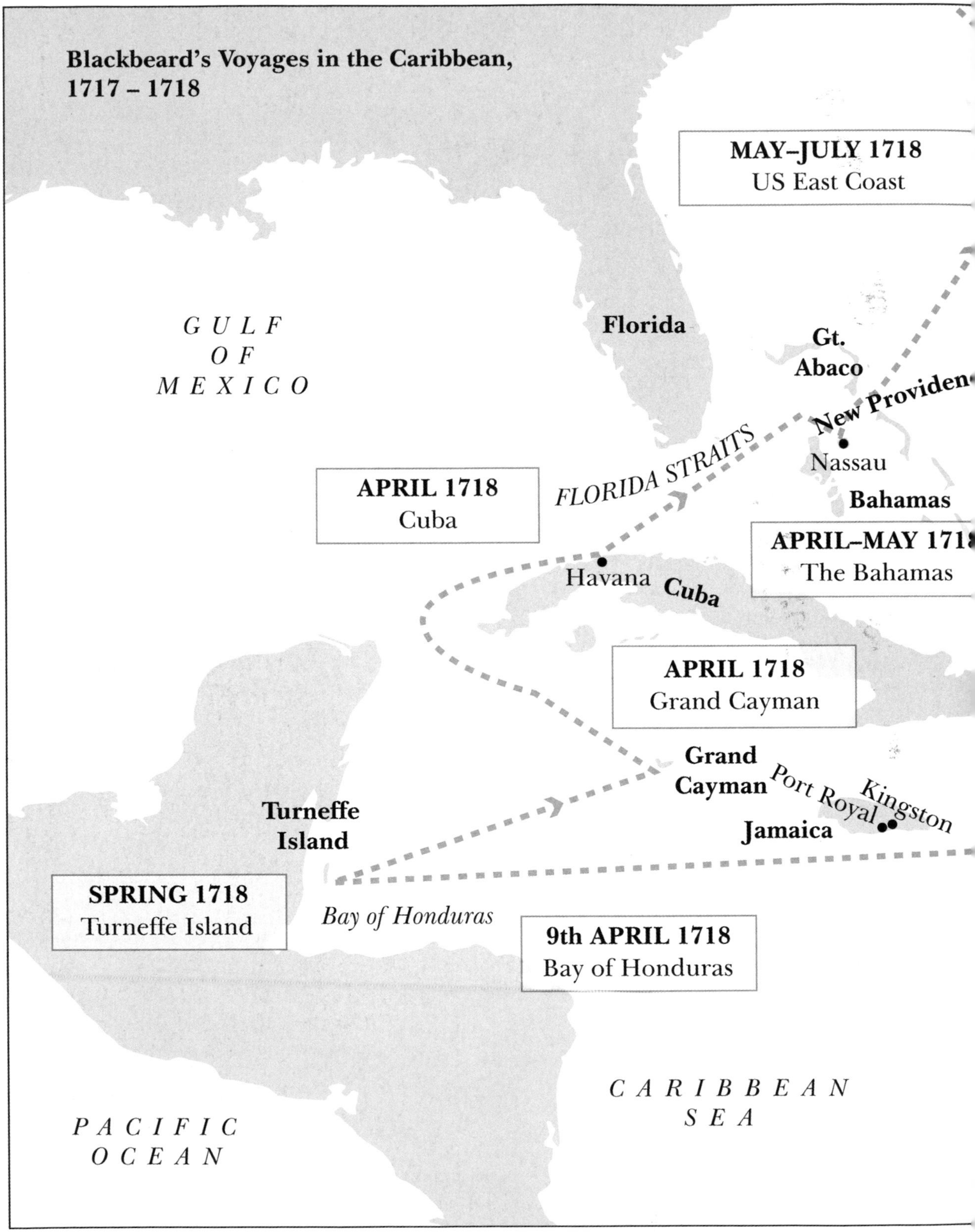

Blackbeard's Voyages in the Caribbean, 1717 – 1718

G U L F
O F
M E X I C O

Florida

MAY–JULY 1718
US East Coast

Gt. Abaco

New Providen[ce]

Nassau

FLORIDA STRAITS

APRIL 1718
Cuba

Bahamas

APRIL–MAY 171[8]
The Bahamas

Havana **Cuba**

APRIL 1718
Grand Cayman

Grand Cayman

Port Royal **Kingston**

Jamaica

Turneffe Island

SPRING 1718
Turneffe Island

Bay of Honduras

9th APRIL 1718
Bay of Honduras

C A R I B B E A N
S E A

P A C I F I C
O C E A N

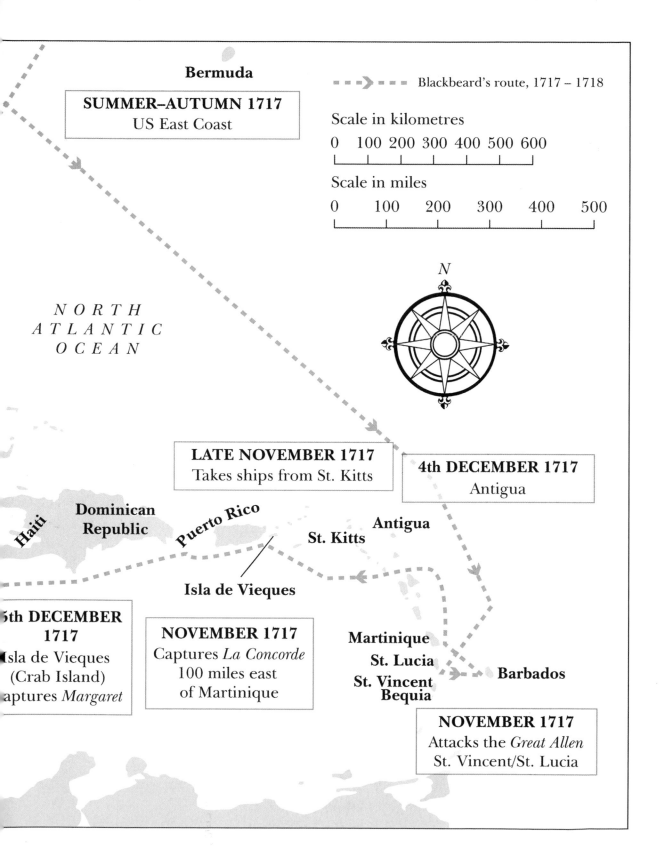

Bermuda

SUMMER–AUTUMN 1717
US East Coast

┈┈▶┈┈ Blackbeard's route, 1717 – 1718

Scale in kilometres

0 100 200 300 400 500 600

Scale in miles

0 100 200 300 400 500

N

*NORTH
ATLANTIC
OCEAN*

LATE NOVEMBER 1717
Takes ships from St. Kitts

4th DECEMBER 1717
Antigua

Haiti

**Dominican
Republic**

Puerto Rico

St. Kitts

Antigua

Isla de Vieques

**5th DECEMBER
1717**
Isla de Vieques
(Crab Island)
Captures *Margaret*

NOVEMBER 1717
Captures *La Concorde*
100 miles east
of Martinique

Martinique
St. Lucia
**St. Vincent
Bequia**

Barbados

NOVEMBER 1717
Attacks the *Great Allen*
St. Vincent/St. Lucia

Prologue

For ten years during the early eighteenth century, the Caribbean was terrorized by a host of ruthless pirates who, more than at any other time, seized ships and cargoes at will and severed trade links that were the life-blood of a fledgling empire. But of all the thieves and thugs active during the so-called Golden Age of Piracy (1716-26), few were more fearsome than Edward Thatch, the 'cruel hardened villain' known as Blackbeard.

It is not known who first gave Thatch his infamous nickname, but there is no doubt that it arose within his own lifetime, conjuring up an image of a man considered to be 'bold and daring to the last degree, [who] would not stick at perpetrating the most abominable wickedness imaginable', as described by his contemporary Captain Charles Johnson. Johnson's detailed impression of Thatch begins with his 'remarkable, black ugly beard':

> which, like a frightful meteor, covered his whole face and frightened America more than any comet that has appeared there a long time. This beard was black, which he suffered to grow of an extravagant length; as to breadth it came up to his eyes. He was accustomed to twist it with ribbons, in small tails, after the manner of our Ramillies wigs, and turn them about his ears. In time of action he wore a sling over his shoulders, with three brace of pistols hanging in holsters like bandoliers; and stuck lighted matches under his hat, which, appearing on each side of his

Captain Teach commonly call'd Black Beard. Engraving by James Basire after Thomas Nicholls, *c*.1730.

face, his eyes naturally looking fierce and wild, made him altogether such a figure that imagination cannot form an idea of a Fury from Hell to look more frightful.

One ship's captain remembered Blackbeard as 'a tall, spare man' – an unembroidered eye-witness description that supports many knee-trembling references to a giant of a man, a devil in disguise. A devil he might have been by reputation, but the man himself was conventionally human.

A thief who carried out acts of mindless destruction, Blackbeard nevertheless had the intellectual ability to develop intricate strategies. Treacherous and unpredictable, he possessed the charisma and physical presence to lead the hundreds of hardened seamen who manned his heavily armed flotilla. Yet his rough ways were softened by a capacity to charm, and although no educated gentleman, he had the energy and ambition to learn to read and write. Indeed in an age when violence was commonplace, he frequently did no more harm to captured captains than to detain them for a while.

Nevertheless Blackbeard had a love of excess (he is said to have had fourteen wives) and many of his victims suffered an ordeal from which they never physically, emotionally or financially recovered. More than any other captain, he exploited their terror through a demonic reputation that he encouraged as much as possible. But while the truth is that he did not actually kill as many men or capture as many ships as some of his rivals, the legends still survive intact – which is why more than 280 years later he is almost the only pirate who remains a household name.

What his reputation is, where it stems from, and how he came to acquire it are questions that will take us to the heart of an enigmatic and complex man. The things he did, and how they eventually proved to be his undoing, are here explored through a fresh appraisal of surviving contemporary documents. Today we might associate pirates with peg-legs, parrots and dreamy tropical islands – but the disturbing truth is the stuff of nightmares.

James Purefoy as *Blackbeard: The Real Pirate of the Caribbean*.

The Mystery of Captain Johnson

Edward Thatch was one of several larger-than-life sea captains indulging in piracy in the Caribbean who would have been lost to history had it not been for the work of one man. In 1724 Captain Charles Johnson published *A General History of the Robberies & Murders of the Most Notorious Pirates*, a collection of short biographies that was ultimately extended to include more than twenty individuals, including Blackbeard. From Robert Louis Stevenson to J. M. Barrie, writers have borrowed extensively from this book, which is regarded as one of the most complete contemporary accounts of piracy and is still in print today.

Yet one of the biggest mysteries in the history of robbery at sea is the identity of Captain Johnson. His maritime knowledge suggests he was a seaman, while his familiarity with Government records indicates that he was well connected. Claims made in the 1930s that the name was a pseudonym used by Daniel Defoe were dismissed in the 1980s. Unless attributed to another person, the majority of quotes that appear in the prologue and the following chapters are from Johnson.

Parts of the records that Johnson himself quoted from have been published as the *Calendar of State Papers, Colonial Series, America and West Indies*, a copy of which is available in The National Archives in London, where the actual records themselves are also kept. Letters from Navy captains are similarly held at The National Archives, while logbooks left by their lieutenants are preserved at the National Maritime Museum, Greenwich. All three sets of documents shed much light on the history of Blackbeard.

Money and Treasure

From the Elizabethan sea-dogs to the Cuban pirates of the 1820s, the glittering lure of silver and gold remained the single biggest motivating factor in piracy. Men hunted such treasure with varying degrees of success, and kept whatever else they happened to find along the way. The truth is, however, that most ships did not then, and do not now, roam the world's oceans weighed down by precious metals and gems.

Merchant vessels were designed to carry a huge range of often mundane bulk commodities, and in the early eighteenth century these included wheat, timber, indigo, cocoa, animal skins, molasses, barrels of pork, sails, cloth, spirits, flour, gunpowder, candles, ivory, sugar, tobacco – and slaves. All of these things were of interest to pirates, who needed food, drink and equipment as much as any other seamen venturing into open waters in all weathers.

All vessels carried a small amount of money in coin and a few, particularly Spanish ships, carried vast quantities of wealth in bullion. The most common coins (or 'pieces') found in the Caribbean in this period were worth eight Spanish *reales* and came to be known as *pesos* or 'pieces of eight'; today one of these silver coins would be equivalent to about £15. Gold coins were called *escudos*, and a coin worth eight *escudos* was known as a 'doubloon'. Gold also appeared as gold bars or as gold dust, while solid silver took the form of plate, bars or ingots. Today, the New York Stock Exchange still trades in fractions borrowed from pieces of eight.

The Origins of a Legend

Little is known for certain about Blackbeard's early life, but it is believed that he was born around 1680. Three-quarters of the contemporary documents give his real name as Edward Thatch, while others refer to him as 'Tatch' or 'Teach'. This probably springs from the difficulty some of his associates from mainland Europe and West Africa had in pronouncing the 'th' sound.

It is probable that Thatch came from an English port, traditionally identified as Bristol. There are suggestions that he came from other places, including London, Philadelphia and even Jamaica, but the significance of all these possible options is that they share one thing in common: proximity to the sea. It is clear that Thatch understood all aspects of shipboard life – a vast subject which required years of experience to master. As a young man he became a successful leader of sailors who in many cases would have been at sea since childhood, and he would never have been able to command their respect if he himself had not gained solid experience of ships at an early age, literally 'learning the ropes'.

It is also probable that Thatch had some education. He must have been able to read and write, since no ship's captain, pirate or not, would have lasted long without having mastered the art of navigation, which requires basic literacy. It appears that the young Edward Thatch was a bright boy, a natural leader and a forceful personality, who grew to be a tall, imposing figure of a man.

We might imagine the young Thatch standing on a quayside, gazing at some of the hundreds of ships moored around him. In Bristol, vessels clustered at many points along the River Avon, 'their masts as thick as they can stand by one another'. Ships were (as they still are) by far the biggest mobile objects made by man, and to a young lad in the late seventeenth century they must have seemed like floating cathedrals.

At the time, Bristol was one of Britain's biggest centres of Atlantic trade. In the medieval centre of the old city, merchants

Broad Quay, Bristol.
Oil painting by
Philip Vandyke, *c*.1760.

sought good prices for their cargoes of sugar and slaves while haggling around bronze trading-tables that still exist today. Beyond the well-to-do trading quarters were squalid areas of little lanes, described by Daniel Defoe as lying 'close and thronged'. Here could be found small ale-houses where seamen swapped tall tales of life at sea in the West, where the warm waters were impossibly blue and Spanish treasure ships were ready for the taking.

A young lad arriving on the River Avon quays would have found himself jostled by dozens of people hurrying beside lines of waiting vessels. He may easily have encountered red-faced workmen dragging heavily laden sledges without wheels – fighting for space with men rolling barrels full of provisions – and traders, selling everything from fish to knives, touting for business among a crowd that included old tars looking for their land-legs again, fresh-faced topmen preparing for the long voyage ahead, and stern-faced boatswains seeking hands to complete their crew. For many boys, asking such people for work would be a daunting prospect. But for the lad destined to become a ruthless pirate captain, strength of character was not in short supply.

Mast and rigging. Still from
Blackbeard: The Real Pirate of the Caribbean.

A wooden world

If Thatch stopped to watch the crew of an armed merchantman preparing for a transatlantic voyage, he would have seen a self-contained wooden world with masts six storeys tall, representing the cutting edge of the period's technology. Within a few decades, English dockyards would be producing men-of-war that represented the maximum feasible size for wooden ships. Vessels such as Nelson's *Victory* were directly descended from the biggest Royal Navy ships in service during the 1690s.

The *Victory* is constructed from up to 6,000 trees, ninety per cent of them oak – the equivalent of 100 acres of woodland. Its twenty-six miles of ropes and cordage supported 6510 square yards of sail, which is more than twice the size of a modern football pitch. The ship that Thatch first sailed on, although very much smaller, would have been built and operated in a similar way and would have been no less bewildering to a boy who had not yet been to sea.

In the dark depths of a merchantman moored on the quay, there would have been men working to fill the cavernous hold, the ship's own warehouse. In order to make sure the vessel sat in the correct position in the water, heavy stones or piles of gravel – known as ballast – were laid down first. On and around these, spare anchors, masts, ropes, sails, timbers and gun barrels would be lowered by enormous pulleys, along with hundreds of barrels containing enough provisions to supply scores of men for three months or more.

Above the hold there might be a deck running the length of the ship, which supported twenty or so guns. Here on the gun-deck most of the ship's men would eat, sleep, banter, and do all the things they would do on shore, except with considerably less room and nothing in the way of privacy. Above their heads were the weather decks, which were permanently exposed to the elements. At the back ('aft', in seaman's terms) was the quarterdeck where in later years the ship's wheel would be found (at this point ships had a more basic 'whipstaff' arrangement connecting directly to the tiller). Ahead of the quarterdeck lay the 'waist', and beyond this, at the front of the ship, was the forecastle (pronounced *fo'c'sle*).

Working aloft. Still from the television film.

When looking at a ship, Thatch would possibly have been impressed most by the three masts towering vertically above him, each capable of supporting a mass of sails. The modern eye might see three apparently separate columns, but to the sailors of Thatch's day the masts were the supporting foundations of a single area of the ship, connected by a bewildering arrangement of ropes and simply known as 'aloft'.

The men involved in raising or lowering the sails could find themselves working 100 feet above the ship, and would expect to do so at any time of day or night in all types of weather. To keep the ship on course, horizontal beams (known as yards) running across the masts could be turned to allow the sails that were attached to them to make the most of

British Sailors Boarding an Algerine Pirate. J. Fairburn's engraving of corsairs, early nineteenth century.

BRITISH SAILOR'S, BOARDING, AN ALGERINE PIRATE.

the shifting winds. By hauling on ropes, the crew operated the yards and raised and lowered the sails. The major ropes, which had a combined length of at least three miles, were all named and included stays, halyards, shrouds and braces. Not all ships were as big as this, but even on a smaller vessel there was an enormous amount for a novice to learn – and it was essential that he learn everything, since the life of a sailor might one day depend on his experience and expertise.

The lure of the sea

Why did Thatch choose to go to sea at all? What was there for him on land? Apparently not enough to keep him there. Besides, the country was at war, always a magnet to restless young men. In 1689 the political fault-line that divided Protestant England from Catholic France erupted in a conflict that was to last, on and off, for more than a century, ending only with the defeat of Napoléon. The opening act, the War of the League of Augsburg, revolved around trade and sea power. Sailors were much in demand as Europe's leading states skirmished in the Channel and Mediterranean while seizing what they could elsewhere.

Much was up for grabs. A New World had come to prominence in the West, promising riches to whomever got there first. Although most of the hundreds of specks of land along the eastern edge of the West Indies offered little in themselves, the European powers had an interest in using them to dominate the surrounding sea-lanes. These led towards the shores of bigger places, full of hope and plenty: Jamaica, Hispaniola (now Haiti and the Dominican Republic), Cuba and the Spanish Main – the name given to Spanish-held territory in Central and South America and the adjacent coastal waters.

But as England battled to assert her dominance in the Caribbean, the Navy was short of ships and seamen. Vessels were fitted out by enterprising men and licensed by the State under 'letters of marque', which entitled their crews to raid enemy shipping for profit. These ships, being privately owned, were known as 'privateers', and were manned by sailors who were not paid by the Navy but instead were offered a share of the plunder from the ships they captured.

Next page: Barbary pirates attacking a Dutch Fleet, by Pietersz Verschuier Lieve, *c.* 1670.

21

There was nothing new in this idea. Muslim privateers, branded as pirates by Christian states, had been plundering ships in the Mediterranean since at least the mid-sixteenth century. Described as corsairs, they operated from North African ports dotted along what was known as the Barbary coast. These seamen were feared for the agility of their vessels (or galleys), their barbarity, and for enslaving their Christian prisoners who were

The Spanish Armada destroyed by Captaine Morgan. From a contemporary engraving of 1685.

The Spanish Armada destroyed by Captaine Morg

forced to work both ashore and at sea – notoriously as galley slaves. The term 'corsair' also came to refer to the Knights of St John, based in Malta, who in the name of religion attacked the Muslims and raided their shipping.

Beyond the Mediterranean, robbery at sea was endemic during the colonization of the Caribbean. Here, in the sixteenth and seventeenth centuries, England (Great Britain after 1707), France, Spain, Portugal, the Netherlands and Denmark attacked each other on land and at sea in official wars and unofficial raids in their attempt to acquire and develop territories. Many of the seamen taking part in these actions had lived among the indigenous people of the island of Hispaniola and learned from them the art of cooking over a barbecue, or *boucan*. From this term, these men, led by charismatic adventurers such as Henry Morgan, came to be called 'buccaneers'.

Buccaneers and privateers in the Caribbean shared a similar identity. In both cases sailors signed up to a 'cruise', agreeing to share the risk as well as the prize. Any plunder was to be divided among the entire crew and, equally, no one could expect to be paid if nothing were captured. Unlike the merchant service, where paid seamen did as they were told while a merchant financier reaped the profit, buccaneering and privateering voyages were considered to be joint ventures and as such, the men could expect to influence a captain's decisions.

On the whole, English buccaneers remained loyal to their country, which in gratitude turned a blind eye to their excesses. During lengthy periods of war, privateer captains (sometimes including former buccaneers) went one step further, in that they were actually granted a recognized form of legal authority. The documents they carried, signed by English officials, allowed them to act on behalf of the State and they could, and did, fly the English flag. Such men were not criminals operating outside the law but were enterprising sailors making the most of the Government's need for help in return for the promise of loot. Once the war was over, however, the letters of marque expired. Anyone who continued to indiscriminately attack ships without the protection of the law was no more than a thief – and a thief at sea was known as a pirate.

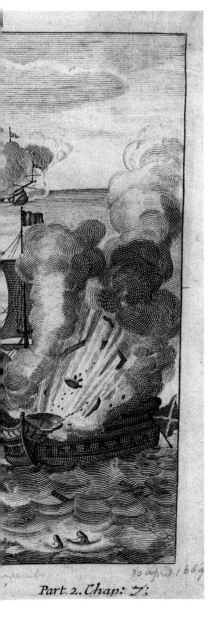

Part. 2. Chap: 7.

Pirates advertised their lawlessness in the form of a black flag and stole whatever they could from anyone they found. In so doing, they left no doubt as to what they were about: they had stepped beyond the law and freed themselves from authority. As outlaws they were united in freedom and therefore different to all other men, whom they dismissed as weak fools too timid to join them.

At the end of the seventeenth century, the potential rewards – even for law-abiding seamen – were greater than most sailors could ever hope to acquire in peacetime. Privateering offered the chance of wealth, and captains had no difficulty in finding or motivating crews. Edward Thatch would not have been slow to see his opportunity.

Capt. Hen Morgan before Panama wh. he took from the Spaniards, from Captain Johnson's *History of Highwaymen*, 1734.

Struck by a Storm

As solid as ships appeared to be, a wooden hull rarely lasted more than fourteen years. Long before its life-expectancy expired, a vessel's timbers began to work loose through its action at sea, forcing the ship's carpenter to carry out a daily round of inspections and repairs. Only then could he reassure the captain that his was a 'tight ship'. Even so, water continually collected in the bowels of the vessel, where it stagnated and gave off a nauseating stench. Rain and heavy spray permeated every inch of the ship so that in rough weather nowhere was dry. Manually operated pumps allowed excess water to be cleared, but using them was exhausting work that sometimes lasted hours at a time. During heavy weather those spared the dismal task of pumping kept an eye on the horizon.

Ominous dark clouds developing above waves whipped by the wind were ignored by a crew at their peril. Moderate waves could soon grow into a swell that eventually broke over the bow. Lookouts on the forecastle were ordered to safety on the foretop (the platform high up on the fore-mast), and from there they shouted down directions on the state of the sea that were passed back to the helmsman. Once the racing winds had covered a boiling sea with foam, a gale had officially become a storm. The crew had to work quickly to bring in canvas, leaving just one or two sails partially set in the hope that they could lie-to – in other words, ride out the worsening weather at the cost of being blown before the storm. Even then the ship could veer so far off course that the howling wind caught the wrong side of her sails, threatening the safety of the masts. In drastic cases the masts were cut away by the crew to prevent them crashing down without warning. The topmen would frequently be sent aloft to check the condition of the masts, the shrouds and the furled sails, for if the wind were allowed to pick away at an exposed corner of canvas, it could rip the sail from the yard. Securing heavy, wet canvas in storm-force winds in the dark, high above the deck, was terrifying work and occasionally a man slipped from the yards. He either plunged into the water where in a storm he would be lucky to be spotted, or else fell onto the deck, suffering serious injury or worse.

To try to prevent deck hands being washed overboard, lifelines were strung horizontally along the length of the deck and a lifebuoy was towed behind the vessel, as in an emergency there would be no time to launch a boat. Even men sheltering below were not safe. If one of the ship's guns broke free of its ropes the crew were faced with a loose cannon which, if not brought under control, could be fatal. One account describes how a gun 'broke away from the tackles and after several sends between the ship's sides ... the gunner's mate lost his leg and ultimately his life'. Someone would have to go after the slithering gun carriage, which might weigh around two tons, and jam its wooden wheels with rolled-up hammocks, 'as playing leap-frog on a see-saw under a shower with the certainty of death if you missed'.

Navigation

The art of arriving at an intended destination by sea was a complicated business. Navigation was the responsibility of a ship's master, who could read and write and used an array of charts, tables and instruments to help him in his work. In the early eighteenth century, pinpointing latitude (how far the ship was above or below the equator) was relatively straightforward. This was done with an instrument called a backstaff that was used to measure the angle of the sun above the horizon at midday.

This was only one half of an essential equation; the other half lay in finding a ship's longitude (the distance covered in an east-west direction), which was much more difficult. This involved comparing local time with the time at the ship's home port – an impossibility in Blackbeard's day, since clocks easily lost time at sea. The solution involved a process of 'dead reckoning' which took into account a ship's compass reading and speed (expressed in knots), both of which were measured at regular intervals using an hourglass. Navigation was made harder still by inaccurate charts, and often sailors were forced to rely on local knowledge. Many trusted the lore of the sea – for example, the presence of certain birds or insects indicated that land was not too distant. In 1720 Captain Roberts's crew missed their destination at the Cape Verde islands and were forced to follow the trade winds back across the Atlantic. Johnson wrote that when they ran low on provisions 'many of them drank their urine, or sea water'.

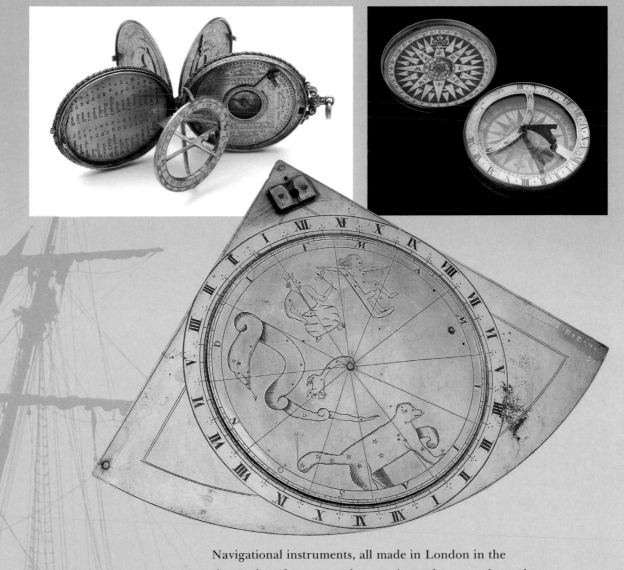

Navigational instruments, all made in London in the
sixteenth and seventeenth centuries and commonly used at sea.
Clockwise from top: an astronomical compendium, a brass-bound
compass dial and an horary quadrant.

CHAPTER

A Voyage into Piracy

If Edward Thatch did go to sea in his early teens or even younger (which would not have been unusual), he might easily have crossed the Atlantic aboard a privateer during the War of the League of Augsburg in the 1690s, when England and Spain fought together against the French. We know, for example, that four well-armed privateers left Bristol in 1694, including the *Charles II*, commanded by a Captain Gibson. Fitted out by a group of London merchants led by Sir James Houblon, the ships were ordered to interrupt the French smuggling trade in the West Indies. First, however, they were to wait at the Spanish port of La Coruña for their orders.

Frustrated by this delay, the first mate of the *Charles II*, Henry Avery, led a mutiny, and quietly put to sea while Gibson was incapacitated. The captain later told a court that at the time he had been 'very ill of a fever', although Johnson claimed Gibson was 'one of those who are mightily addicted to punch'. After putting Gibson in a small boat Avery took command and set sail for Madagascar. Once in the Indian Ocean, he joined forces with two smaller vessels and successfully attacked the *Ganj-i-Sawai*, a powerful 40-gun ship which belonged to the Great Moghul of India and carried a cargo of 500,000 silver and gold coins. Avery's men stole the lot, horribly abused the women passengers and escaped with £1000 each, in a raid that amounted to one of the biggest hauls in pirate history. Such stories quickly passed around the ports and harbours of the Atlantic. Perhaps on Thatch's first voyage, the older hands may

Capt. Avery and his Crew taking one of the Great Mogul's Ships. Etching after William Tett, eighteenth century.

Willm Telt delin   W^r Pritchard sculp
CAP^t. AVERY and his Crew taking one of the GREAT MOGUL'S Ships

have tried to impress their new recruits with fabulous tales like this, as sailors always did.

What duties would a young seaman have been expected to carry out? As a ship's boy, his work would range from turning the hourglass to mucking out the ship's livestock, and depending on his captain, he might even get a little tuition. He might be taught some basic navigation and how to read and write. A boy might also be used as a messenger and would quickly come to know the entire ship and its crew.

When the vessel was in action, the young Thatch might have served on the gun-deck as a powder-monkey. Gunpowder was too dangerous to

Right: A New Map of Asia, by John Ogilby, 1673.

Below: Captain Avery receiving three chests of Treasure on board of his Ship. Woodcut, from Captain Johnson's *History of the Pyrates.*

Captain Avery receiving the three chests of Treasure on board of his Ship.

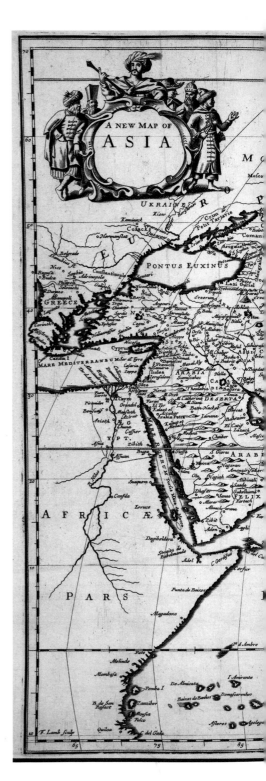

be kept on the deck itself, and dozens of small barrels were sealed inside the magazine, a strong-room inside the hold. Throughout the fighting the powder-monkeys collected bags, or 'charges', of powder from the magazine, then ran the length of the ship giving them out to the gun-crews. Dark and claustrophobic, the magazine was always a dangerous place to work. Its position near the waterline protected it to some extent from enemy shot, but accidental sparks could cause an explosion that would instantly rip the vessel apart. Life was worse when the boys returned to the gun-deck, where they encountered enemy fire, recoiling guns and deafening noise amid clouds of choking smoke.

For a tall lad like Thatch, working in the cramped gun-deck with around five feet of headroom would have been especially difficult. An alternative for the youngest and ablest of the ship's crew was working unsupported on the highest yards stretching out from the top of the mast, as so-called 'topmen'. Skilled sailors who were responsible for keeping the ship on course, topmen enjoyed a reputation for being able to carry out their tasks in all types of sea conditions. Even just climbing aloft involved some terrifying manoeuvres: at one point the seaman found himself hanging virtually upside down beneath the 'top' as he hauled himself over the edge of the wooden structure now popularly (though mistakenly) known as the 'crow's nest'. In fact, a perfectly accessible gap was cut into the timbers so that a man could easily climb through the platform, but this was dismissed as 'the lubber's hole', used only by novices and soft-hearted men more used to farming than sailing. Having proved that he had a head for heights, a lad like Thatch would take his turn furling sails in a squall or keeping a weather-eye open as a lookout. In the meantime, he would practise scores of different knots, and learn when and how each was best used about the ship.

Privateering

As a sailor Thatch would have found that his skills were 'a universal Passport, that renders him welcome, and finds him ready Money in almost every Corner of the Globe', as the seaman known as Barnaby Slush put it in 1709. Experienced

Right: The Jack-of-all-trades. *No. 1 Cabin-Boy*, drawn by Thomas Rowlandson, 1799.

Rowlandson delin.

Marks sculp.

No. 1
CABIN-BOY.

London Pub.^d Feby 16 1799 by R. Ackermann, 101 Strand

men could expect to serve aboard any type of vessel. Thatch's contemporary John Young went to sea at '14 or 15 years of Age' and in 1710 listed the ports he had visited, as noted by the maritime historian Marcus Rediker. Young 'sailed from London to Barbados and Jamaica, fought aboard three West Indian privateers, went "sugar-droghing" in the Caribbean coastal trade, found his way on a merchant ship back to London and then in various voyages saw Bristol, the African coast, Virginia, Lisbon, Genoa, Leghorn, and Cartagena'.

In 1697, the war against France came to an end and privateers could no longer operate legally – until 1702 when a new conflict began in Europe, sucking in all the major powers. At stake lay succession to the powerful Spanish throne, and the conflict stretched to the Americas, where Spain's enormous empire was unrivalled. The War of the Spanish Succession left English ships vulnerable to attack from both the French and the Spanish, and since the Royal Navy still had insufficient vessels, the Admiralty once again turned to privateers to help protect – and expand – English interests. Twelve were commissioned in Bermuda, and a further eight in Jamaica. Cruising between the islands of the Caribbean, rarely far from wild game or fresh water, privateer crews exploited their expert knowledge of local winds and currents in their hunt for the enemy. They were well aware that the easiest place to capture a ship was in a narrow stretch of water hemmed in by rocks and reefs – and a classic example of this, the Florida Straits, lay on the treasure ships' route home to Spain.

It is at this point that the story of Edward Thatch can begin to be documented with some certainty. The privateer captains included Benjamin Hornigold, a respected man of whom it was later said that 'most people spoke well of his generosity'; but whatever his own virtues, his crew included several men who went on to become notorious pirates, among them Thatch and the charismatic Sam Bellamy. They patrolled the shipping lanes of the West Indies aboard a sloop named the *Mary Anne*, armed with eight guns, and (according to Johnson) Thatch 'often distinguished himself for his uncommon boldness and personal courage', though he 'was never raised to any command'.

Pirates seizing a ship: French pirate Jean Lafitte and crew boarding the *Queen* East Indiaman, from a nineteenth-century book on piracy.

A step too far: piracy

Since the idea of stepping beyond the law was largely dismissed by privateers, it is a mistake to think of them as simply 'legally sanctioned pirates', though their French and Spanish victims might have thought differently. Men like Benjamin Hornigold had every reason to embrace the rule of the Establishment. It was the Government that sanctioned their actions, it was the colonial governors who sheltered their ships, and it was the High Court of the Admiralty that paid out on anything they captured under the Prize Act of 1692. They saw themselves not as 'different', or separate, as pirates did, but as an extension of the Navy – loyal subjects of the Crown who were simply making a living in the manner that had been honestly offered to them. Pirates cared nothing for the Crown and did as they pleased, calling their lawlessness freedom.

Everything changed for the crew of the *Mary Anne* when peace came in 1713. Hornigold, having been the master of his own fortune, could not bring himself to give up his independent life once the war was over. Other captains felt the same; in the words of George Lowther, 'it was not their business to starve, or be made slaves'. Telling a captured captain that they had not consented to the Articles of Peace with the French and Spanish, Hornigold and his crew continued to pursue their old enemies.

With these unsanctioned attacks, they descended into piracy – not that Hornigold saw it that way. He insisted that the crew 'meddle not with the English or Dutch'. But Sam Bellamy was less squeamish: he had seen the freedom and riches that were on offer, and no one was going to get in his way. With the support of most of the crew, he deposed Hornigold, setting him adrift in a boat alongside anyone else who didn't have the guts to go on the piratical 'account' – among them Edward Thatch.

Sam Bellamy and the Whydah

O n 26 April 1717, the *Whydah* galley, a former slave ship, was caught in a storm near the perilous sandbanks off Cape Cod. Aboard were 146 pirates under the command of the notorious Sam Bellamy. The 300-ton *Whydah*, a three-masted vessel, had once brought 700 slaves from the West African coast to the Americas. Captured in February, now the *Whydah* was Bellamy's flagship and carried bags of silver and gold accumulated from more than fifty prizes, in addition to the riches it had had on board when Bellamy seized it: ivory, indigo, sugar, pieces of eight, doubloons, gold bars and pouches of gold dust, later valued at between £20,000 and £30,000.

After a furious north-easterly wind sprang up, waves thirty feet high eventually drove the vessel onto a sandbar, where she was battered by the sea until some of her twenty-eight cannon toppled over and smashed through the deck onto the men sheltering below. As she began to break up, according to Johnson, the pirates rounded up anyone in the crew who had not joined voluntarily and then 'murder'd all their prisoners, that is, all their forced men'. Only two survivors reached the shore, where they found themselves surrounded by mutilated bodies piling up in the surf.

In 1984 maritime archaeologist Barry Clifford discovered the wreck of the *Whydah* just a quarter of a mile from the shore, along with more than 200,000 artefacts, including 8000 silver coins, gold (bars and dust), pistols, dinner-ware, African jewellery, clothing, cannon and a bell inscribed 'The Whydah Gally 1716'. There is probably more to come, since everything recovered so far amounts to between six and twelve per cent of the wealth the crew claimed to have had.

It is impossible to put a modern value on such a glittering hoard of artefacts retrieved from what is the world's only confirmed pirate shipwreck, but together the information they provide on sea robbers and their way of life is priceless. Ornate pieces of Akan gold jewellery were broken up so that the metal could be fairly distributed. Pirate fashions are revealed by the discovery of metal buttons, cuff-links, collar stays, rings, neck chains and square belt buckles. A pistol with ornate brass scrollwork, together with a three-foot silk ribbon attached to its handle, might have belonged to Bellamy himself – or perhaps to the man whose leg bone was found, complete with a silk stocking and a small black leather shoe.

In 2000 Barry Clifford's team discovered five more shipwrecks. While exploring the harbour of Ste Marie, a tiny island off the north-east coast of Madagascar, divers found the remains of various boats, including one believed to be Captain Kidd's *Adventure Galley*. Archaeologists have recovered rum bottles and shards of Ming porcelain dating from the Kidd era, and further explorations are planned.

The Wickedest City on Earth

The bewitching blue waters of the Caribbean were no less idyllic in the eighteenth century than they are now. The turquoise lagoons lapping over coral reefs must have been a feast for the eyes of English sailors, more used to the cold waters of Europe's seas. Many men had had a taste of exotic lands while sailing the Mediterranean, a region that fell under the stern eye of the Royal Navy and where vessels were vulnerable to Muslim corsairs. But here in the Caribbean, instead of corsairs there were Spanish treasure ships, and the Admiralty was at least two months away, offering a sense of freedom not to be found in Europe.

English commerce in the Caribbean was once dominated by the town of Port Royal, which occupied a prominent position on the island of Jamaica and at one time was one of the richest ports in the colonies. Jamaica's economy had been built by thousands of slaves who worked in harsh conditions on the island's plantations, producing sugar that was partly refined for shipping home or else locally distilled into rum. In the 1660s, Port Royal's well-protected harbour had hosted Henry Morgan's buccaneers, but in later years it was used by hundreds of merchants.

Many lived in stone buildings on the waterfront, squeezed in among bustling taverns and gambling dens along with brothels offering girls such as Mary Carleton, said to be as 'common as a barber's chair'. In between bear-baiting and cock-fighting, a sailor could find all the 'foul vices' he desired in the 'wickedest city on earth', as Port Royal came to be called. This was no New England town founded on religion and morality but a seaman's haven on the western frontier of the European wars, where life was cheap with no questions asked. And then suddenly, on the morning of 7 June 1692, most of the town was sent crashing into Kingston Harbour by a devastating earthquake that claimed the lives of around 5000 people. Of those who survived, many were left with nothing. John Pike, a joiner, told his brother that 'I lost my wife, my son, a 'prentice, a whitemaid and six slaves and all that I ever had in the world'. The town was rebuilt, but it never completely recovered, and by the time Edward Thatch first saw Port Royal (probably in the mid-1690s), many of the 3000 residents were living across the harbour in the new town of Kingston.

The Port Royal earthquake,
7 June 1692, as depicted in a
contemporary report.

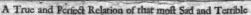

A True and Perfect Relation of that most Sad and Terrible

EARTHQUAKE, at Port-Royal in JAMAICA,

Which happened on *Tuesday* the 7th. of *June*, 1692.

Where, in Two Minutes time the Town was Sunk under Ground, and Two Thousand Souls Perished: With the manner of it at Large; in a Letter from thence, Written by Captain *Crocket*: As also of the *Earthquake* which happen'd in *England*, *Holland*, *Flanders*, *France*, *Germany*, *Zealand*, &c. And in most Parts of *Europe*: On *Thursday* the 8th of *September*. Being a Dreadful Warning to the Sleepy World: Or, God's heavy Judgments shewed on a Sinful People, as a Fore-runner of the Terrible Day of the Lord.

The EXPLANATION.

A. The Houses Falling. B. The Churches. C. The Sugar-Works. D. The Mills. E. The Bridges in the whole Country. F. The Rock and Mountains. G. Captain Ruden's House Sunk first into the Earth, with his Wife, and Family. H. The Ground rolling under the Minister's Feet. I. The great Church and Tower Falling. K. The Earth Opening and Swallowing Multitudes of People in Morgan's Fort. L. The Minister Kneeling down in a Ring with the People in the Streets at Prayers. M. The Wharf covered with the Sea. N. Dr. Heath came from Ship to Ship to Visit the bruised People, and do his last Office to the dead Corpses that lay Floating from the Point. O. Thieves Robbing and Breaking open both Dwelling Houses and Ware-Houses during the Earthquake. P. Dr. Trapham, a Doctor of Physick, hanging by the Hands on a Rock of the Chimney, and one of his Children hanging about his Neck feeing his Wife and the rest of his Children a Sinking. Q. A Boat coming to save them. R. The Minister Preaching in a Tent to the People. S. The dead Bodies of some Hundreds floating about the Harbour. T. The Sea washing the dead Carkasses out of their Graves and Tombs, and dashed to pieces by the Earthquake. V. People swallow'd up in the Earth, several as high as their Necks with their Heads above Ground. W. The Dogs eating of Dead Mens Heads. X. Several Ships Cast away and driven into the very Town. Y. A Woman and her two Daughters beat to pieces one against the other. Z. Mr. Backford his Diging out of the Ground.

Port-Royal, in *Jamaica*, *June* 30. 1792.

SIR,

THIS with my Respects to all our Friends, comes amidst an Inundation of the deepest Sorrow, to bring you the Dreadful Account of our Misery and Trouble, tho' I presume that before this the unwelcome Tydings are arrived at your Ears, of the Dreadful and Terrible Earthquake which happen'd here on *Tuesday* the 7th. of this Month. About half an Hour after Eleven a Clock in the Morning, the Earth suffer'd a Trepidation or Trembling, which in a Minute's time was increased to that degree, that several Houses began to tumble down, and in a little time after the Church and Tower, the Ground Opening in several Places at once, Swallow'd up multitudes of People together, whole Streets sinking under Water, with Men, Women and Children in them; and those Houses which but just now appeared the Faireft and Loftiest in their State, and might vie with the finest Buildings, were in a Moment Sunk down into the Earth, and nothing to be seen of them; such Crying, such Shrieking and Mourning I never heard, nor could any thing in my Opinion, appear more Terrible to the Eye of Man: Here a company of People Swallow'd up at once; there a whole Street Trembling down; and in another Place the trembling Earth opening her Ravenous Jaws, let in the Mercileft Sea, so that this Town is become a heap of Ruines; Captain *Ruden's* House was one of the first that Sunk, with him, his Wife and Family, and several others in it: We have an Account from St. *Ann's*, that above a Thousand Acres of Wood-land are covered with the Sea, Destroying many Plantations; tumbling down most of the Houses, Churches, Bridges and Sugar-mills throughout the Country; so that those who have lived their Lives here till all they had, I could only balance my self for one, who have left my Ship, and very considerably other ways, but I am very well satisfied because it is the Lord's Doings.

In this dreadful Concussion several Ships in the Harbour, were drove into the Town and loft one whereof was a *French* Prize, which was drove into the Market place, and there loft. We reckon by the Dreadful Account which is given, that about two Thousand People, Men, Women and Children was loft in this Town. Dr. *Trapham*, a Physician in this Place, were Miraculously faved, by hanging by the Hands upon the

Rock of a Chimney, and at of his Children hanging about his Neck, were both faved by a Boat; but his Wife and the rest of his Family and Children, were all Loft: Several People were Swallow'd up of the Earth, when the Sea breaking in before the Earth could Close, were washed up again and Miraculously faved from Perishing: Others the Earth received up to their Necks, and then Closed upon them and fqueez'd them to Death with their Heads above Ground, many of which the Dogs Eat; Multitudes of People Floating up and down, having no Burial. The Burying Place at the Palisadoes is quite Destroyed, the dead Bodies being washed out of their Graves, their Tombs beat to Pieces, and they floating up and down; it is fad to think how we have Suffer'd: The Earth hath still fits of Shaking, with very much Thunder and Lightning and dreadful Weather; yet this had so little effect upon some People alas, that the very fame Night they were at their Old Trade of Drinking, Swearing, and Whoreing; breaking open Ware-houses, Pillaging and Stealing from their Neighbours, even while the Earthquake lasted, and several of them were destroyed in the very Act; and indeed this Place has been one of the Lude in the Christian World, a Sink of all Filthiness, and a meer Sodom.

Dr. *Heath*, the Minister of the Place, has Labour'd very much, being continually employed in Burying of the Dead, Christning of Children, Preaching and Praying with the Bruised, Wounded, and Dying People, going from Ship to Ship to do his Office, as well as to Shore: He has Preached fo effectually and powerfully, and laid open the hainoufnefs of Sin fo well, that many of the Old Reprobates are become New Converts; those that us'd to Mock at Sin, Now Weep bitterly for it, and People fawing in great Numbers to Hear him; and indeed he is much to be Commended, and deserves Praise from every one, having discharged his Duty like a good Shepherd. The Morning on which the Earthquake happen'd was very Serene, not shewing the least Symptoms of the Dreadful Earthquake which Succeeded. The Town is most part of it already come'd by the Sea, and will in a short time I believe be wholly under Water; for those Houses which remain, daily fall to Pieces, the Ground yielding under them. We have not yet a compleat Lift of those loft; but these taken Notice of most, are, Attorney General *Musgreve*, Provost Marshal *Reeve*, My Lord Secretary *Reyner*, Captain *Ruden* and his Family, Captain *Agar*, Doctor *Beyes*, Captain *Wails*, Captain *Woods*, and his Family, Mr. *Nuffold* and his Family, Mr. *Croffe* Family, Mr. *Alincke* Family,

Captain *Whiffin* and his Son, Mrs. *Robinfon*, Mrs. *Gifford*, Doctor *Trapham's* Family, Mrs. *Fuller*, Mr. *Eynne*, Mr. *Bourne*, Mr. *Stephenne*, Mr. *Rytee* and his Wife, Mr. *Pryer*, Mr. *Lewdifport*, Mr. *Atwell*, Mrs. *Radburn* and her Family, Mr. *Rynes* and his Family, Mr. *Will. Turner*, Mrs. *Moflen* and his Family, Mrs. *Eefpine* and her Child, Mrs. *Elizabeth Brackford*, Sir *James Coffeigh's* Daughter, Mrs. *Deerington's* Child, Mr. *Dennigh*, Captain *Coniege*, Captain *Dawrie*, Captain *Morrice*, Captain *Child*, Mr. *Wooly*, Mr. *Naffi*, Mr. *Moores*, Mr. *Geo. Phillips*, Mr. *Norberye's* Wife, Mr. *Jonathan Wood*, Mrs. *Crofee*, Colonel *Ream*, Colonel *Reeve's* Lady, Mr. *Maytraus*, *Job's* Child, Mr. *Dggins*, Captain *Whiffen*, Mr. *Stockyano* and his Family, Mr. *Reybe*, *Knight's* Widow and Neece, Mrs. *Sweetwater*, Mrs. *Susannah Carfon*, Mr. *Kyrne*, Mr. *Hollowerthen* and his Family, Mr. *John Lake* and his Wife, Mr. *John Eyth's* Wife and Child, Mr. *Harmer* and his Family, Mr. *Drane*, Mr. *William Turner*, Mr. *Haine*, and Mr. *Backford's* two Daughters.

Reader, Since the aforefaid dreadful Earthquake in *Jamaica*, one has been felt nearer to us, (viz.) On *Thursday* the *Eighth of September* it was in the Camp before *Dunkirk*, at which the Mostly as he sat at Dinner in an Old House, that all to it felt it: It was at the fame time felt at the *Hague* in *Holland*, where it made the Bells for in the Steeples; as also at *Paris*, and feveral other places in *France* and *Germany*; few Places in *Europe* efcaping the dreadful Effects thereof: In *England*, at *London*, *Chatham*, *Street*, *Rochefter*, *Sheernefs*, *Portfmouth*, and other Places: And at *Middleburgh* in *Zealand*, it continued for fome time, and was most violent in still Weather; it caused the Earth, to move like the Waves of the Sea, that the People in the Streets were fenfibly hold by which ever they went with in few themfelves: The Sea had the fame fate, for the Ships were thrown up and down; And the People were afraid that the Steeple of the Abby by its motions would have tumbled down; it caused the Bells to strike one against another; And many of the Inhabitants in the Night fled into the Fields, and feme into the Country much damage was done to the Top of the Houses, Chimneys and Windows, &c. The like has been in *Brabant*: But we blefs God, it did no Harm that we hear of: Then let this be a Warning to us to forfake our ill Courfes and turned our Lives, left Almighty God fhould deal with us as he has done with thofe in *Jamaica*. *Amen*.

Licensed and Entered according to Order.

London, Printed by R. Smith, and are to be Sold by G. Croom, at the *Blew Ball* in *Thames-ftreet*, near *Baynard's-Caftle*: And William Miller, at the Acorn in St. *Paul's* Church-yard, Where Gentlemen and others may be furnished with most forts of Acts of Parliament, Kings, Lord Chancellors, Lord Keepers, and Speakers Speeches, and other forts of Speeches and State-Matters; as also Books of Divinity, Church Government, Humanity, Sciences &c.

View of Port Royal, Jamaica, by Richard Paton, *c.* 1758.

3
CHAPTER

Out of Control in the Bahamas

The end of the War of the Spanish Succession brought a sudden expansion in trade, and with it a change in official and public attitudes to men who lived by looting ships. Piracy in any form was not to be tolerated. This opinion even extended to the antics of former privateers like Benjamin Hornigold who claimed that they only attacked their former enemies, and nothing illustrates this better than the experience of Captain Henry Jennings. On 31 July 1715, ten Spanish galleons heavily laden with treasure were engulfed by a devastating hurricane in the Florida Straits. The battered fleet, sailing home to Spain, could do nothing to avoid the treacherous reefs south-east of the mainland, and once caught in shallow waters the ships began to break up. As they vanished into the sea, they took with them more than 1000 people and a cargo of bullion and silver worth seven million pieces of eight. The loss of this fleet stands as one of the worst disasters in Spanish maritime history.

A salvage crew was sent to retrieve the sunken treasure chests, and as tales of storehouses full of gold and silver spread around the Caribbean, scores of men sailed to Florida looking to steal what they could. In Port Royal, Jennings disguised his true intentions by obtaining a commission to hunt for pirates before he, too, set a course for Florida.

Jennings was described as an educated man 'of good understanding and good estate'. One sailor caught by him said he was treated gently, receiving generous payment for the twenty gallons of rum looted from his vessel. Jennings commanded respect among privateer financiers and was given two ships, three sloops and 300 men for his expedition. In January 1716 the Englishmen drove off sixty Spanish soldiers and escaped with 120,000 pieces of eight in an attack worthy of the buccaneers themselves.

On their return home they captured a Spanish ship and plundered another 60,000 pieces of eight before jubilantly entering Port Royal, flushed with success. But far from receiving the welcome he might have expected, Jennings found that he had fallen out of favour. When the Spanish complained about the bullion raid, the Government in London ordered Jennings's friends in Jamaica to issue an order for his arrest.

Things had come a long way since the reign of Elizabeth, when Englishmen plundering the Spanish Main received official support, albeit covertly. The wealthy backers of Francis Drake included the Queen herself, who knighted him on the deck of his ship after his return from a hugely profitable raiding voyage in 1580. The buccaneers a century later were also sanctioned by those in power, and many 'continually found favours and encouragers at Jamaica', as Johnson wrote. But the peace that followed the War of the Spanish Succession nourished a growth in trade that was cosseted by treaties and diplomacy, and pirates who fed upon this newfound success were regarded with loathing and disgust.

England, after all, had been fighting for most of the period between the beginning of the War of the League of Augsburg (1689) and the end of the War of the Spanish Succession (1713) – that is, twenty-one out of twenty-five years. When trade finally resumed, merchants and officials in Britain and the Caribbean fought to ensure that it was protected.

The islands in the West Indies served as stepping-stones in a widely cast trade network that reached far-flung corners of the world such as Calcutta, Boston and Port Royal. Colonial expansion at this time was not about nation-building but more to do with developing new territories that promised fortunes to those who didn't die of disease. And now that England's chief rivals, Spain and France, had lost the war, nothing could stop a giddy expansion of trade. Except piracy.

Map of the Caribbean and coasts of America, by Joan Olivia, 1640.

Pirates grabbing the profits posed a direct threat to this new-found economic recovery and they were consequently viewed with a sense of revulsion. Sea robbers were labelled 'hellhounds', and 'vermin' who were *Hostes Humani Generis* ('enemies of all mankind'), 'full of Malice, Rage and Blood'.

Some privateers-turned-pirates, such as Henry Jennings and Benjamin Hornigold, promised not to capture English ships. But even attacking the Spanish 'and other nations in amity with His Majesty' risked compromising valuable trade agreements such as the *asiento*, Britain's newly acquired contract to sell slaves to Spanish America. For this reason, all manifestations of piracy were condemned. Forced to flee from Port Royal, Jennings sailed back towards the wrecked treasure ships and established himself on the nearest English-held land, the Bahamas. Here, in the ramshackle town of Nassau, he was joined by other former privateer captains and their crewmen – including Benjamin Hornigold and Edward Thatch.

The Flying Gang

The 700 islands of the Bahamas, scattered over 100,000 square miles of the western Atlantic, offered plenty of fresh water, fish, turtles and wild game. They were owned by a small group of British absentee landlords, the Lords Proprietors (whose ancestors had been granted land in the Americas by Charles II), who felt powerless to stop the frequent attacks on the islands by the Spanish so didn't bother to try.

A Spanish galleon being attacked by pirates, by Andries van Eetrecht, seventeenth century.

49

The Towne of Puerto del Principe taken & sackt
Part 2: Chap: 5.

50

The Towne of Puerto del Principe taken & sackt, after an attack by Henry Morgan's buccaneers in 1668.

One of the most important islands was New Providence, which offered a perfect refuge for pirates. It had a sparkling natural harbour with a smaller island at its entrance flanked by two sandbars, which prevented heavy warships from approaching Nassau, a small town perched on the waterfront. To protect their perfect location, the pirates mounted several guns in a fort overlooking the harbour.

The 200 English families who were still trying to scratch a living on the islands felt they were losing their struggle against the combined forces of the Spaniards, tropical storms and pirates. Between 1702 and 1716, eight official reports described the 'miserable condition' the Bahamas were in. The settlers believed they had been abandoned in a place that was fast becoming, as one put it, a 'recepticall and shelter of pirates and loose fellows'.

Drinking in makeshift wooden taverns alongside local traders, the pirates felt themselves to be beyond the reach of the law. They did not live in anarchy, but adopted a loose code of rules inspired by the buccaneers' egalitarian spirit. This code established a sense of unity among the group and was upheld by an informal council of captains led by Jennings. Occasionally the men declared a vague intention to create 'a second Madagascar', where a virtual pirate colony had been carved out of the forest during the 1690s. As remote as Madagascar is, the seamen managed to trade with the occasional merchant ship while living a life of freedom among the indigenous people. The pirates in New Providence, however, posed a greater threat to trade, since they were closer to major shipping lanes used by heavily laden vessels that could be captured by fast sloops. They 'call themselves the Flying Gang', wrote one former resident.

Both Jennings and Hornigold acquired reputations as 'gentleman' pirates that still persist today. On one occasion Hornigold captured the crew of a sloop, but, as a passenger reported, 'did us no further injury than the taking most of our hats from us, having got drunk the night before … and toss'd theirs overboard'. Nevertheless, in Nassau pirate captains either could not or would not stop their men 'plundering the inhabitants, burning their houses and ravishing their wives', forcing many of the settlers to leave.

Reports received in Jamaica spoke of excesses also committed at sea, including one case where pirates dumped three unwanted crewmen into a fishing boat, 'first whipping them inhumanely and burning matches between their fingers, ears and toes'. They whipped a fourth member of the crew who was just a boy of 12, and hanged a fifth, while a sixth was so severely beaten that when thrown overboard he was unable to swim and drowned as the pirates watched. The British Commander-in-Chief in Jamaica, General Peter Heywood, noted that after vessels had been captured the pirates sometimes 'murdered all the people', took what they wanted from the cargo, destroyed the rest, then burnt the ship.

'Forced to go a pirateing'

The expanding threat of piracy seriously alarmed colonial authorities from New England to Barbados. General Heywood warned that pirates were 'putting a stop' to trade between Jamaica's merchants and the Spanish, while letters written by the Lieutenant-Governor of Virginia, Alexander Spotswood, included tales told by terrified islanders who had fled to his colony. Spotswood feared the 'nest of pirates' in the Bahamas was growing, and he was right.

By the spring of 1716, more and more were making their way there. Marcus Rediker has estimated that during the following two years, between 1800 and 2400 pirates were operating in the region. Captain Johnson believed them to be so 'formidable and numerous' that 'English merchants ... suffered more by their depredations than by the united force of France and Spain', and modern historians have since shown he was correct.

Who were these men? The historian David Cordingly has found that just over half the pirates active from 1715 to 1725 were English, Scottish or Welsh. Almost all the others came from the American or West Indian colonies, though there was a scattering from Sweden, Holland, Spain, Portugal and France. They were almost without exception experienced sailors who had formerly served in the Royal Navy or the merchant service,

The buccaneer of myth and legend, as illustrated by Howard Pyle in his *Book of Pirates*, 1921.

or aboard privateers; thus they shared a common identity and vocabulary, talking of clewlines and reefing, catheads and crossjacks, in speech so technical as to be a 'language by itself'.

As well as sharing a seafaring past, they dreamt of a similar future that included wealth, freedom and hope. However, such things lay beyond the reach of common sailors – except for pirates, who were 'Princes to [seamen] … exempt from the General Toil...', as the sailor 'Barnaby Slush' wrote in 1709.

One of the biggest causes of this expansion in piracy was the reduction of the Royal Navy. Rediker has found that after the war ended in 1713, the Navy plunged from 49,860 men to just 13,475 within two years – a huge surplus of unemployed maritime labour that came just as the economy began to slow down. Although the export of colonial goods, previously interrupted by the war, picked up with the arrival of peace, by 1715 exports were falling, and seamen who had earned up to fifty-five shillings per month in 1707 now made half that amount. It was hard for a sailor to find work, and those who did were poorly paid and harshly treated.

For the crews of privateers who had spent years chasing the high life, things had fallen a long way from the freedom they had once known. 'Since the calling in of our privateers,' the governor of Jamaica wrote in a letter to London, 'I find already a considerable number of seafaring men at the towns of Port Royal and Kingston that can't find employment, who I am very apprehensive, for want of occupation in their way, may in a short time desert us and turn pirates.' Hundreds did indeed 'turn pirate', though not all of them willingly. Stephen Smith from Jamaica insisted he was 'forced to go a pirateing for to gett a living, which is much against my will'. To men like Smith, Nassau was a town where traders could be found who were known for 'inriching themselves by sideing and dealing with, entertaining and releiveing such villians who … resort there to sell … their piraticall goods', as one resident, Thomas Walker despairingly put it. Walker, a tough sea captain who had forcefully tried to stop the pirates' excesses, was forced to flee Nassau prior to March 1716 after Hornigold 'and others of his Society' threatened to shoot him.

With the extra recruits came new opportunities, and Thatch was not one to hold back. By early 1716 he had his own command, as recorded by a Captain Mathew Musson. While visiting the island of Great Abaco in the Bahamas, Musson discovered settlers who had fled from New Providence, among them Thomas Walker. They told him that five pirate captains 'made Providence their place of rendezvous', including

Blackbeard on deck. Still from the television film

Hornigold, who instead of the 140 men he had once commanded now had just eighty. Another captain they identified was a man called Thatch who had seventy men and a sloop of six guns. When Thatch left Hornigold's command he apparently took half the crew with him, though it seems there was no ill feeling, as contemporary documents show they subsequently sailed together in 'consortship'.

Out of control

In the summer of 1717, while in Nassau, Thatch stumbled across the Caribbean's most improbable pirate, Major Stede Bonnet. Described by Johnson as a rich and educated man, Bonnet filled his cabin with books from his house on Barbados; and unlike other pirates, who traditionally captured their sloops, Bonnet paid for his, naming it the *Revenge*. As an army officer-turned-plantation owner, he made a poor sea captain, and by the time Thatch met him he was recovering from injuries suffered in an optimistic attack on a Spanish man-of-war which had claimed thirty to forty of his men. Perhaps it was with some relief that Bonnet and his crew accepted Thatch's offer to take over the *Revenge*. That summer they sailed north to the American colonies, accompanied by a second sloop commanded by Hornigold.

On 29 September, Thatch captured the *Betty* of Virginia. The pirates took what they wanted, including wine, then sank the ship along with the rest of the cargo. On 12 October, a pirate sloop called *Revenge*, carrying 150 men and twelve guns and commanded by an Edward Teach, stopped a vessel in the Bay of Delaware which was carrying 150 passengers from Liverpool. A newspaper article referring to this incident mentions that aboard the sloop was a Major Bonnet, who 'walks about in his morning-gown'.

Around this time Thatch plundered at least another six vessels in the area, including the *Robert*, a sloop from Philadelphia, and a ship named the *Good Intent* bound for Dublin, all 'of which met with most Barbarous inhumane Treatment', reported the *Boston News-Letter*. When Thatch stopped another, commanded by a Captain Farmer from

Jamaica, his haul was typical of most pirate robberies – not gold and silver but Farmer's 'Mast, Anchors, Cables and what money was on board'. Another account refers to the theft of a 'New Suit of Sailes and Rigging'. When Thatch captured Captain Pritchard from St Lucia, he took a cargo of sugar and 'most of their clothes'.

By the autumn of 1717 it appears that Thatch had developed an interest in acquiring a bigger and more powerful ship. When he captured the *Sea Nymph*, a two-masted merchant vessel known as a 'snow', he ordered the crew onto a second captured ship and kept it for himself. Sailing for Portugal in October, the *Sea Nymph* had recently cleared Philadelphia when the pirates seized it; they dumped her cargo of wheat into the Atlantic before allowing her crew to escape.

The *Sea Nymph* apparently did not come up to the expectations; not long afterwards he attacked a Captain Goelet and forced him to take the snow in exchange for his sloop. The pirates threw Goelet's cargo of cocoa overboard before releasing him, and as he resumed his journey to New York he saw Thatch plunder two further vessels.

Contemporary accounts for this period only mention Hornigold twice, compared to at least five references to Thatch (occasionally identified as 'Teach'), and of the two men it is clear which was the most notable. By the autumn of 1717, the pupil had become the master. As the raids continued, colonial governors from Virginia to Barbados urged the Council of Trade and Plantations in London to curb the growing menace of piracy. Eventually the Council noted that 'the pirates are grown so numerous' that without effective action 'the whole trade from Great Britain to those parts will be in imminent danger of being lost'. Though they had finally recognized that piracy was getting out of control, the authorities were too late to stop the worst excesses, as Thatch was about to show.

Pirate Sloops and Ships

Vessels used by pirates were virtually always stolen rather than purpose-built. In searching for a ship, sea robbers looked for certain qualities, and most of their vessels were variations on a theme. A ship had to be fast enough to outrun a 'prize', and light enough to negotiate the narrow inlets and shallow bays ably exploited by pirates when hiding from the heavier vessels used by the Navy. For these reasons, the majority of pirate crews chose sloops, which were small, streamlined craft with one mast. Weighing up to eighty tons, a typical pirate sloop might be armed with a dozen cannon.

In pursuit of prestige and firepower, however, some pirate captains aspired to bigger vessels, as Edward Thatch showed when he took over the two-masted 'snow' *Sea Nymph*. Other vessels with two masts might be more accurately described as 'brigs' or 'brigantines'. In the early eighteenth century, only vessels with three masts could properly be described as ships.

As anarchic as a pirate ship might have appeared to be, its crew still experienced the same harsh realities of life at sea encountered by all sailors. There were times when they needed to be organized and if they were to outrun their prey they needed to be better than most. As an example of this, pirates would frequently run their vessel onto a deserted beach in order to clean the hull. In a laborious process known as careening, the crew unloaded the craft and hauled it over on one side before scraping off the barnacles and weed that slowed their vessel's progress in the water. This work was carried out more regularly by pirates than by merchant crews or the Navy, giving them a distinct advantage in speed.

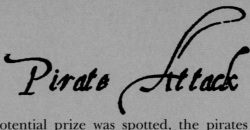

Pirate Attack

Once a potential prize was spotted, the pirates initially simply shadowed her. Dozens of scarred and sunburnt men leered at their potential victims, sizing up the opposition and hoping to intimidate a vulnerable crew. Eventually the merchant captain was instructed to board the pirate vessel and surrender his ship: when Captain Skinner encountered the pirate Edward England off Sierra Leone he was 'ordered to come on board in his boat, which he did'. Few merchant ships carried enough men or guns to defeat the pirates, though they might try to outrun them.

When a chase began, the pirates' boatswain tried to get every inch of speed out of the ship by reeling off instructions to the men working aloft. Garrat Gibbens, a boatswain who served with Blackbeard, was responsible for making the vessel sail as efficiently as possible. A boatswain worked closely with the master, the ship's senior navigator, who used charts and instruments to set a course agreed by the crew.

Once a merchant ship had surrendered, pirates sent across a boarding party led by the quartermaster. They could stay aboard for hours, even days, searching the vessel, taking what they wanted and often destroying the rest. 'They tore up the hatches and entered the hold like a parcel of furies,' Johnson says of Bartholomew Roberts's crew, 'and with axes and cutlasses cut and broke open all the bales, cases and boxes ... more like fiends than men.'

Finding a Flagship

Edward Thatch's rampage along the coast of the American colonies in the autumn of 1717 had been monitored by the *Boston News-Letter*, the region's only regularly issued newspaper. On 4 November the paper reported that Captain Teach and his crew were heading for the 'Capes of Virginia in hopes to meet with a good Ship there, which they much wanted'. Thatch finally found a vessel big enough to match his ambition when he spotted *La Concorde* on 17 November, around 100 miles east of Martinique. At the time no other pirate commanded anything as powerful – such a ship would show the likes of Hornigold that Thatch was in a league of his own.

La Concorde, a slave-ship rife with disease, had been at sea for more than three months. In the depths of the 200-ton vessel, 455 people lay chained in a wretched state on dark, airless decks that reeked of human waste. Slaves were not the only commodity that the ship's captain, Pierre Dosset, had bought during his stay on Africa's Gold Coast. He and his second-in-command, Lieutenant François Ernaud, had also invested in something that was intended to safeguard their future, something that they had concealed from the men – or so they believed. In fact, a sailor called Louis Arot had seen what they had bought and where they had hidden it. It was a grave responsibility for a ship's boy of fifteen, the youngest member of the crew.

Researchers – including John de Bry, Jacques Ducoin and members of North Carolina's *Queen Anne's Revenge* Shipwreck

A Slave Ship, painted by William Jackson, *c.* 1780. The ship is British, but slaves were seen as a valuable commodity and were traded extensively throughout the eighteenth-century world.

Project – have shed much light on the history of the *Concorde*. It is believed to have been built in Nantes, one of France's biggest slaving ports; and was owned by René Montaudoin, whose family was heavily involved in the trade. He had sent the *Concorde* from Nantes to West Africa on 24 March 1717, armed with sixteen cannon and manned by a crew of seventy-five. On 8 July she sailed from Whydah (modern-day Ouidah in Benin) with 516 slaves bound for Martinique, where labour was needed for the sugar plantations. Since then, exhaustion, scurvy and dysentery had taken their toll, and not only among the Africans. By the time the *Concorde* arrived in the Indies, sixteen sailors had died and another three dozen were ill. Strong though it seemed, the weakness of its crew made the ship all too vulnerable to the two pirate sloops that were stalking it.

Carrying twelve guns and 120 pirates, the *Revenge* could have fired a crippling broadside at the *Concorde*. But a battered ship was of no value to a greedy pirate crew, and as was his habit, Thatch relied on intimidation through superiority of numbers. Together, the *Revenge* and a second sloop of eight guns carried a force of up to 250 men. Dosset knew that in a straight fight his exhausted men would not stand a chance, and when the *Revenge* fired a couple of warning shots, he struck his colours and surrendered his vessel.

The new recruit

The pirates took the *Concorde* to the island of Bequia, south of St Vincent, where they landed the French crew and the slaves. Apart from her human cargo, the vessel at first glance appeared to be carrying little of value, but Thatch was sure there must be something more. In an attempt to force them to talk, Dosset and Ernaud were beaten and warned that their throats would be cut unless they revealed where the ship's money was kept.

Bequia was the first dry land that fifteen-year-old Louis Arot had seen in months. This was not Africa where white boys easily succumbed to disease – here was a beautiful Caribbean beach. The Englishmen who had brought him here did not seem to have dysentery or scurvy, nor did they appear to be in a hurry; instead they had freedom and rum. Arot volunteered to join them, knowing he could offer something that would instantly sweeten their opinion of him. He revealed that while in Africa the ship's senior officers had bought about twenty pounds of gold dust – and he told the pirates where it was hidden. In addition to the gold, which today would be worth around £100,000, the French officers had amassed money, silver plate and jewellery. Here at last was the kind of gleaming prize that pirates dreamt of.

The Englishmen allowed Arot to join the crew along with three other volunteers. To them, a lad like Louis made an ideal recruit. Here was a low-class boy who knew little besides the sea and took risks to better his own life – someone, in fact, not much different to themselves. Any new recruit, however, was regarded with suspicion until he had signed up to the pirate code, or 'Articles of Regulation'. These varied from ship to ship but generally emphasized equality in an attempt to prevent 'disputes and ranglings'. Those who signed up agreed to a set of rules by which they lived or died, and in return each man was given a fair share of the loot and an equal vote on major decisions, such as the course of the ship. The pirates held councils that were powerful enough to sack an unpopular captain, and in this way created democracies that were decades ahead of their time. When Howell Davis, who terrorized the West African coast, drew up articles, he made a speech that included a conviction shared by many pirates, 'the fun of which was, a declaration of war against the whole world'.

New recruits were always useful, but what Thatch needed most were skilled hands. He told Dosset that he had decided to keep another ten men, including three surgeons, two carpenters, a pilot, a caulker, a cook, a gunsmith and a musician, along with some of the slaves – and the ship itself. The remainder of the crew were dumped into Thatch's smaller sloop and left to make their way to Martinique. By the time they arrived at the French colony, they had renamed the boat *Mauvaise Rencontre* – 'Bad Encounter'. Later, Dosset and Ernaud each wrote an account of their final voyage on board the *Concorde* detailing how they lost their ship to Blackbeard.

The power of piracy

The capture of the *Concorde* elevated Thatch's men to a position of power enjoyed by few pirate crews. Blackbeard had come a long way since his days as a privateer, and at around this time he parted company with his old captain, Benjamin Hornigold. Johnson suggests that Hornigold gave his 'consent' to Thatch keeping the *Concorde*, but this version of events is unsupported

A Piratical Vessel, destroying a Merchant Ship. Engraving from *The West India Pirates*.

A Piratical Vessel, destroying a Merchant Ship.

by other documents, including the depositions from Dosset and Ernaud. While the French officers mention 'Edouard Titche', they make no reference to Hornigold, much less offer any suggestion of him deciding who would or would not keep such a powerful ship. It is probable that Hornigold was not present at the capture of the *Concorde* at all, but in Nassau, where he was soon to abandon piracy altogether.

To Hornigold and Jennings, piracy was about getting rich, preferably at the expense of the French or Spanish. Having seized what they wanted, there was no sense in endlessly testing the patience of the authorities; instead they intended to retire and enjoy their ill-gotten gains. But to a younger generation of thieves, including Edward Thatch, there was more to piracy than gold. In robbing ships of his own nation, in threatening to cut the throats of simple seamen and in commanding something the size of a small warship, Thatch showed that, for him, piracy was also about power.

He cared nothing for his country. The queen he had fought for, Anne, had died in August 1714 and her place had been taken by George of Hanover – who, it was believed, could not speak a word of English. Many pirates sneered at such a monarch. Dismissing him and the British Establishment that accepted him, they looked towards an alternative. The political movement that rejected King George in favour of Anne's Catholic half-brother James Edward Stuart was known as Jacobitism and was widely supported by pirate crews, as reflected in the names of some of their vessels, such as *King James* and *Royal James*. Thatch, too, aligned himself with the memory of Anne, whose immediate family had been pushed aside. Believing that she deserved to be avenged – though precisely how is not clear – he named his new ship *Queen Anne's Revenge*, and set out in search of anyone from anywhere.

The horror of the gun-deck

The first person Thatch avenged was not Queen Anne at all, but his old shipmate Sam Bellamy. His victim was Captain Christopher Taylor, commander of the *Great Allen*, a merchant ship from Boston, where six members of Bellamy's crew had

Sailors in a fight. Mezzotint by William Ward after Thomas Stodhard, 16 April 1798, showing gun-crew working in cramped conditions.

been recently hanged. It was in their memory that Taylor was savagely whipped and beaten when he was captured towards the end of November. He was later put ashore on St Vincent while Thatch set his ship alight, delighting in its destruction. Sometimes merchant captains were dealt with in this way if they tried to flee from pirates, or worse still, if they attempted to engage them. As we shall see later on, sea robbers were not afraid to take on heavily armed ships, including men-of-war.

In preparing for a battle at sea in the eighteenth century, seamen would throw sand onto the deck to soak up blood and provide extra grip for their naked feet. The crew of a merchantman trying to outrun pirates might also scatter broken bottles in an attempt to slow down barefoot boarding parties. The most dangerous preparations took place in the magazine deep within the ship. Different-sized bags, designed to supply guns of various sizes, were filled with explosive powder and placed ready to hand. Meanwhile, on the gun-deck, men gathered around the cannon in teams of up to twelve. Discipline and stamina were essential if the gunners were to maintain a maximum rate of fire. A gun-deck was a hot, dark, cramped space where men were easily injured. After a cannon was fired it leapt dangerously backwards until the tackles that tethered it broke the recoil. Once it came to a stop, the first member of the gun-crew would sponge the inside of the barrel with a sheepskin swab, and after every few rounds a second man armed with a handspike would drag out the remnants of wadding that had been packed around the last shot. The next charge would be pushed home – consisting of, for example, four pounds of gunpowder, followed by new wadding. A cannon-ball was then sent rolling down the length of the barrel and held in position with more wadding which prevented the ball moving about with the action of the ship.

A slow-match (a short length of smouldering fuse) was taken from its protective tub and applied to the touch-hole. The powder hissed, then exploded in a deafening crescendo, forcing the ball out of the barrel at 984 feet per second. At this speed a twelve-pound cannon-ball could smash through both sides of a warship 200 yards away. A gunner who was slow or lost concentration could easily be injured by the ricochet of the cannon as it shot back against its ropes. The rolling deck and the deafening noise of the other guns also added to the dangers faced by the crew. Meanwhile, boys – some younger than Louis Arot – repeatedly crept through the thick of the action ready to hand over fresh supplies of powder. If the ship was being fired at, the boys knew there was nowhere to hide, for nowhere was safe.

A 'tall Spare Man with a very black beard'

Throughout the rest of November the *Queen Anne's Revenge*, accompanied by an unidentified brigantine of ten guns and the sloop *Revenge*, sailed towards Jamaica, capturing vessels as they went. By 5 December, having somehow lost their brigantine along the way, the pirates reached Crab Island (now known as Vieques), six miles east of Puerto Rico, where they seized the sloop *Margaret*. The master, Henry Bostock, was held aboard Thatch's flagship for eight hours. He heard reports of the ship's growing hoard of treasure, and saw for himself a quantity of silver plate, including a 'very fine cup' which he was told had been taken from Captain Taylor just a few days earlier. He had ample time to take note of Thatch, whom he later described as a 'tall Spare Man with a very black beard which he wore very long'. While he was interrogated about the movements of other ships in the area, Bostock's sloop was emptied of his 'cargo of cattle and hogs, his arms, books and instruments'. In a letter sent to the Council of Trade and Plantations, Bostock claimed that the *Queen Anne's Revenge* had no fewer than thirty-six guns.

By early 1718 wild tales of a black-bearded monster who sent ships to the bottom of the sea were carried with the trade winds throughout the Caribbean. Captain Johnson claimed that a few days after burning the *Great Allen*, the *Queen Anne's Revenge* encountered the warship *Scarborough* and attacked her in a running battle that lasted several hours. However, this incident does not appear in the *Scarborough*'s log, nor is there a record of it anywhere else, and it is almost certain that it never actually happened. Henry Bostock, whose capture aboard the *Margaret* took place at around the same time, related that the pirate crew 'owned they had met the Man of Warr on this

Station, but said they had no business with her, but if she had chased them they would have kept their Way'.

For Thatch, however, the inaccuracy of the stories whirling about him must have been of little concern. As the most infamous pirate captain in the Caribbean, Blackbeard derived much of his power from a terrifying reputation which he deliberately tried to encourage – wild tales such as the "attack" on the *Scarborough* only served to extend the legends surrounding him, whether they were actually true or not.

'A tall Spare Man with a very black beard'… Still from television's *Blackbeard*.

The Slave Trade

For centuries the maritime history of the Americas revolved around the European slave trade, which in its entirety existed for more than 400 years. Seamen sailed to Africa to collect human beings whom they treated as cargo, chaining them in disease-ridden ships and exporting them to colonies from Brazil to Virginia. As slaves, Africans tended crops such as sugar and cotton, which were shipped back to Europe. These commodities brought profits that were invested in goods which were taken to Africa to buy more slaves.

Much of this triangular trade was driven by educated merchants who lost sight of the 'enlightened' age they were living in as they looked towards establishing family fortunes, which in some cases still exist. Wealthy people such as these, who generally regarded black Africans as inferior savages, shipped up to twelve million men, women and children across the Atlantic in this way. Most were worked into an early grave, and generations of their descendants spent their entire lives living the same miserable existence.

The opinion that pirates had of black men is hard to gauge. Sea robbers adopted a form of democracy based on genuine equality, and Blackbeard had high regard for at least one former slave among his crew, a man named Caesar. Yet he was living in an age when it was accepted that black people could be sold for profit. When Blackbeard captured slaves aboard the *Concorde*, he gave most of them back to the French crew. At one point 60 per cent of the men aboard his ship were black, but it is impossible to say how many of them were treated as equals. It is likely that many of these men were routinely given the hardest or dirtiest jobs on the vessel.

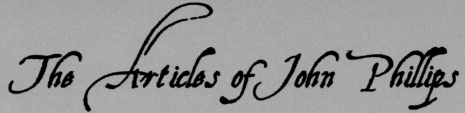

The Articles of John Phillips

1. Every Man shall obey civil Command; the Captain shall have one full Share and a half in all Prizes; the Master, Carpenter, Boatswain & Gunner shall have one Share and [a] quarter.

2. If any Man shall offer to run away, or keep any Secret from the Company, he shall be marroon'd, with one Bottle of Powder, one Bottle of Water, one small Arm and Shot.

3. If any Man shall steel any Thing in the Company, or Game, to the Value of a Piece of Eight, he shall be marroon'd or shot.

4. If at any Time we should meet another Marrooner [pirate] that Man that shall sign his Articles without the Consent of our Company, shall suffer such Punishment as the Captain and Company shall think fit.

5. That Man that shall strike another whilst these Articles are in force, shall receive Mose's Law [39 lashes] on the bare Back.

6. That Man that shall snap his Arms, or smoak Tobacco in the Hold, without a Cap to his Pipe, or carry a Candle lighted without a Lanthorn, shall suffer the same Punishment as in the former Article.

7. That Man that shall not keep his Arms clean, fit for an Engagement, or neglect his Business, shall be cut off from his Share, & suffer such other punishment as the Captain & Company shall think fit.

8. If any Man shall lose a Joint in time of an Engagement he shall have 400 Pieces of Eight; if a Limb, 800.

9. If at any time you meet with a prudent Woman, that Man that offers to meddle with her, without her Consent, shall suffer present Death.

5
CHAPTER

A Floating Den
of Thieves

On the evening of 28 March 1718, a heavily armed ship named the *Protestant Caesar* was cruising alone, more than 350 miles west of Jamaica. Sailing in isolated waters, her English commander, Captain William Wyer, had earlier 'espyed a large Sloop which he supposed to be a Pirate', (as the *Boston News-Letter* later put it) and consequently was keeping a watchful eye out. Once night fell, however, he and his men believed they were safe.

Suddenly, at around 9 p.m., cannon-balls smashed into the stern of their ship accompanied by a volley of musket-fire. When Wyer fired the chase-guns mounted in his cabin, the pirates yelled that if he fired again they would show no mercy. Ignoring the threat, Wyer used everything he had and for three hours his flaming guns roared in the darkness. At around midnight the pirates had had enough and slipped back into the night.

They and their sloop, the *Revenge*, belonged to Blackbeard's flotilla, although he himself was not aboard. At the time of the attack, Thatch was collecting fresh water for the *Queen Anne's Revenge* on the island of Turneffe, off the coast of modern-day Belize. Here he had a stroke of luck when his ship was inadvertently approached by the *Adventure*, an eighty-ton sloop commanded by David Herriot. As soon as he saw the pirates' black flag, Herriot knew that an attempt to flee would be foolish, and after surrendering without a fight both he and his sloop were quickly recruited into Blackbeard's force. Half of Herriot's crew were put aboard the *Queen Anne's Revenge* and Thatch's

Thatch aboard the *Revenge*.
Still from the television film.

navigator Israel Hands was put in command of the *Adventure*. From this point Herriot was sucked into a life of crime that was to end in bloody violence.

Like David Herriot, many men were forced to serve aboard pirate vessels, particularly skilled sailors such as surgeons, carpenters and musicians. When he captured the *Margaret* in December 1717, Blackbeard ordered two men to join him, including Edward Latter, a cooper. However, the vast majority of sea robbers were volunteers, taken on after their own ships had been taken. (John King, a passenger aboard a sloop seized by Black Jack Bellamy, was so determined to join the men who had captured him that 'he declared he would kill himself if he was restrained and even threatened his mother who was then on board as a passenger'.) While twenty sailors might man a typical merchant ship, pirates almost always welcomed new volunteers and their crews had an average size of around eighty. As many hands as possible were needed to overwhelm a potential prize, and furthermore a big crew meant that each man had more time to himself. However, not all volunteers were welcome. Pirates 'entertain'd so contemptible a Notion of Landmen' that few men were recruited who could not tell one rope from another; although married seamen possessed the necessary skills they were sometimes seen as having divided loyalties. Rediker suggests the typical pirate was single, aged around twenty-seven, and a volunteer.

The *Queen Anne's Revenge* was joined by the *Revenge* at Turneffe in early April. On 9 April, they set sail, accompanied by three further sloops, and headed south into the Bay of Honduras, where, anchored close to shore, Thatch found the *Protestant Caesar*. Flying their 'Black Flags and Deaths Heads', the pirate vessels approached the ship, their crews ready for battle.

Blackbeard was at the height of his powers. After carving a course through the Caribbean, he had left in his wake stories of exploits that rippled across the Indies. For five months he and his crew had been living aboard the *Queen Anne's Revenge* and as they prepared for action, his men must have had every confidence in him. It is easy to imagine them swaggering about the ship, their cutlasses swinging as they walked. Beside them, ropes and hammocks may have hung in various states of untidiness while an odd assortment of cannon lay skewed against the gun-ports. Here and there, racks of shot and buckets of sand would have stood beside small wooden tubs containing smouldering slow-matches. Perhaps the smell of alcohol permeated the length of the ship, testimony to the fact that here was a floating den of thieves, out of control and out of reach of the authorities.

Many of the prizes they had captured in the past they had left unharmed, but this was personal. Blackbeard was determined that Captain Wyer 'might not brag ... that he had beat a pirate' and some of his sloops were flying red flags, the traditional signal that no mercy would be shown. Wyer's crew were prepared to take on Spaniards but the sailors refused to face the blood-thirsty pirates they had attacked a few days earlier and 'quitted the Ship believing they would be Murthered'. The terrified men fled for shore, leaving the *Protestant Caesar* to be picked over by Blackbeard's quartermaster, William Howard, and eight other men. Eventually, the vessel, which came from Boston, was burnt in memory of the executed members of Bellamy's crew.

Heading back out into the open waters of the Caribbean, the pirates cruised north-east to the Spanish-held island of Grand Cayman, capturing and abandoning small boats as they went. Passing to the north of Cuba, they sailed first towards Havana and then on to the Bahamas, attracted by the islands' wrecks and the hope of easy pickings. As it approached the pirates' old haunt, three crowded sloops escorted the *Queen Anne's Revenge*. In command of the *Revenge* was Lieutenant Richards, one of Blackbeard's most trusted men; Herriot's *Adventure* had been given to Israel Hands, and a Spanish sloop captured off Cuba was being used as a supply boat. At the time, this was the only pirate flotilla powerful enough to take on all but the biggest naval ships. Unknown to Blackbeard, the number of Navy ships in the region was set to increase as the authorities planned their first major assault on piracy. Already, news had come from London that was to mark the beginning of the end for the renegades in Nassau.

Declaring war against the pirates

By 1717, the governors of New England, Bermuda, Virginia, the Leeward Islands and New York had frequently warned London about the growing threat of piracy. 'Tis with great hazard that ships come to us, which has occasioned a great

Woodes Rogers and his Family, by William Hogarth, 1729. Woodes Rogers is on the right.

scarcity of all sorts of provisions,' wrote the governor of Jamaica in August. At the same time, people closer to home echoed the colonists' fears. More than 160 merchants in Britain warned of the 'neglected condition' of the Bahamas and recommended that Captain Woodes Rogers, a successful former privateer, be sent to the islands as governor.

A tough, no-nonsense sea captain, Woodes Rogers was born in Bristol in 1679 and made his reputation in a three-year privateering voyage that began in 1708. During this expedition, which took him round the world, Rogers captured around twenty French and Spanish ships, including a 400-ton Spanish galleon laden with two million pieces of eight. While venturing into the Pacific Ocean, 350 miles west of Chile, Rogers stopped at the little known Juan Fernández Islands, where he made a discovery that was to inspire one of literature's most popular maritime stories.

A group of seamen venturing ashore encountered a strange man 'clothed in goat-skins who looked wilder than the first owners of them'. The man identified himself as Alexander Selkirk, formerly master of the *Cinque Ports,* who had been marooned in 1704 by a Captain Stradling. After Rogers found Selkirk in 1709, he included a description of him in an account of his privateering voyage published three years later. In 1719 this formed the basis of Daniel Defoe's novel *Robinson Crusoe.*

Rogers's book also gave details of a face-wound he received during a battle fought off the coast of California. He wrote that 'The bullet struck away [a] great part of my upper jaw, and several of my teeth, part of which dropt down upon the deck where I fell.' A few days later he was wounded in the ankle by a wood splinter that knocked out part of his heel bone. Here, Bristol's merchants believed, was a man tough enough to take on the pirates.

Government officials suggested taking the Bahamas out of the hands of their owners, the Lords Proprietors, and handing them over to the Crown, and in September 1717 King George I agreed. He decreed that three extra warships should be sent to the Americas; Woodes Rogers should go to the Bahamas as governor and, most importantly of all, pirates who surrendered were to be pardoned for any crime committed at sea before

5 January 1718. These measures represented the most decisive action taken against sea robbers since the War of the Spanish Succession ended in 1713, and together they marked a turning point in the history of piracy in the Caribbean.

By December 1717, news of the amnesty had arrived in America and the West Indies. Benjamin Bennett, Governor of Bermuda, sent his son to New Providence armed with copies of the royal pardon that 'were accepted of with great joy'. Two ships sent to the island from Jamaica came back with a letter from Benjamin Hornigold declaring that 'Wee embrace HM act of grace and return HM our hearty thanks'. At first, most of the 300 pirates were happy to give up their past ways, and eight of them – including Henry Jennings – personally surrendered to Bennett in Bermuda.

On 23 February 1718, the Royal Navy ship *Phoenix* anchored in Nassau's harbour. Her captain, Vincent Pearse, managed to persuade almost half of the 500 'young, resolute, wicked fellows' he found there to surrender to him, including Hornigold. Other pirates were more hesitant, refusing to give themselves up without an assurance that they could keep their loot. Many were afraid to 'have ventured our necks for nothing', as one told Bennett. This unresolved issue darkened the pirates' mood, and six weeks after Pearse arrived he was told 'to be gone or it should be worse for him'. Some of those who had surrendered went back on the 'piratical account', including Captain Charles Vane. Once Woodes Rogers arrived in the summer he would find that much work awaited him.

A strange man clothed 'in goat-skins' – illustration from *Robinson Crusoe*, 1719, one of the very early editions of Daniel Defoe's classic, based on the real life seaman Alexander Selkirk.

By the King

A Proclamation for Suppressing Pyrates

George R.

Whereas we have received Information, that several Persons, Subjects of Great Britain, have since the 24th Day of June, in the Year of our Lord, 1715, committed divers Pyracies and Robberies upon the High-Seas, in the West-Indies, or adjoyning to our Plantations, which hath and may Occasion great Damage to the Merchants of Great Britain, and others trading into those Parts; and tho' we have appointed such a Force as we judge sufficient for suppressing the said Pyrates, yet the more effectually to put an End to the same, we have thought fit, by and with the Advice of our Privy Council, to Issue this our Royal Proclamation; and we do hereby promise, and declare, that in Case any of the said Pyrates, shall on or before the 5th of September, in the Year of our Lord 1718, surrender him or themselves, to one of our Principal Secretaries of State in Great Britain or Ireland, or to any Governor or Deputy Governor of any of our Plantations beyond the Seas; every such Pyrate and Pyrates so surrendering him, or themselves, as aforesaid, shall have our gracious Pardon, of and for such, his or their Pyracy, or Pyracies, by him or them committed before the fifth of January next ensuing. And we do hereby strictly charge and command all our Admirals, Captains, and other Officers at Sea, and all our Governors and Commanders of any Forts, Castles, or other Places in our Plantations, and all other our Officers Civil and Military, to seize and take such of the Pyrates, who shall refuse or neglect to surrender themselves accordingly.

… the fifth Day of September, 1717, in the fourth Year of our Reign.

George R

A medal commemorating the arrival of King George I in England in 1714
and his dominion of the seas, made by J. Croker.

Pirate Flags

First adopted by Emanuel Wynn in 1700, the black flag was flown throughout the Golden Age of Piracy (from 1716 to 1726). Its nickname, the 'Jolly Roger', was perhaps an Anglicized version of *jolie rouge*, describing the red, or 'bloody', flags which were almost as common and which usually indicated that no mercy would be shown. After 1700 the death's-head symbol (a skull) came to be included on pirate flags, along with other designs associated with death, such as cutlasses, wounded hearts, bones and skeletons. The death's head had been used to signify death since medieval times and appeared on tombs (and later also in captains' logbooks) in the same way that we might write 'RIP' today.

Blackbeard used 'Black Flags and Deaths Heads' as well as a flag showing death in the form of the devil, in a design probably also used by other pirates. The devil, appearing as a skeleton complete with horns, in one hand holds an hourglass signifying the vanishing sands of time, and in the other a spear that pierces a heart from which fall three drops of blood.

Pirates occasionally lulled a victim into a false sense of security by raising a false flag, as Edward Low did in 1723. Approaching a sloop, his men first flew Spanish colours then 'hauled them down, hoisted their black flag, fired a broadside, and boarded her'. When threatened with capture, pirates sometimes destroyed their black colours to avoid the humiliation of being hanged beneath them, as Captain Skyrm's crew did in 1722. Captured by the Royal Navy, the men threw their flag overboard so that it would not 'be displayed in triumph over them'.

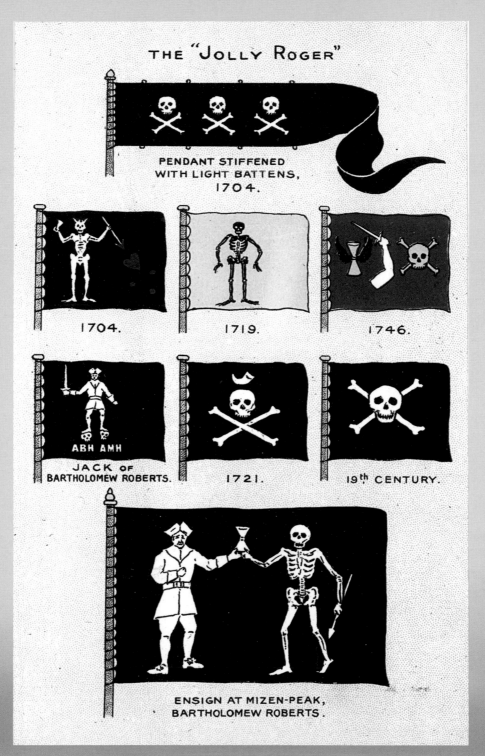

Pirate flags. Blackbeard's is in the second row, far left.

CHAPTER

6

The Siege of Charleston

There is no doubt that Blackbeard knew about the king's pardon, but he had no interest in meeting Captain Vincent Pearse of the Royal Navy. By May 1718 only one thing was occupying his mind. He and his crew needed medicine so desperately that they were prepared to go to unprecedented lengths to get it. It is impossible to be sure about the reason for this but the horrendous disease that came to be called yellow fever sometimes besieged Caribbean ports at this time of year.

Brought to the West Indies by slaves in the 1640s, yellow fever reached Port Royal in 1655 and was soon to be found in many harbours throughout the region. Victims suffered a range of symptoms including fever, vomiting, aching limbs, bleeding from all orifices, liver failure and jaundice – the latter giving rise to the name. The disease is transmitted by mosquitoes, which are frequently found in waterfront towns – particularly during the rainy season which begins in the Bahamas in May. In Thackeray's *Vanity Fair*, Lieutenant Osborne refers to a friend who 'had the yellow fever three times; twice at Nassau, and once at St Kitts'.

Infected mosquitoes could decimate the occupants of damp wooden structures such as a house or a ship. The dank decks of the *Queen Anne's Revenge* had once been filled with hundreds of slaves, many of whom had been racked with dysentery, and in such a vessel disease could easily spread. What Blackbeard and his men needed was a port large enough to provide the medicine they lacked. At this time of year they had previously attacked ships off the American colonies, and the nearest harbour that lay in that direction was Charleston in South Carolina.

The siege begins

Developed by English settlers, colonists from Barbados and French Huguenot refugees, Charles Town, as it was originally known, was the leading port of the Carolinas. Ships from Europe frequently brought essential supplies before returning home laden with cargoes of tobacco, indigo and deer hides. On the bustling quaysides fishermen and deep-sea sailors mingled with wealthy ladies accompanied by planters in powdered wigs, while well-to-do merchants haggled over slaves, rice and cotton.

North and South Carolina were the property of the Lords Proprietors, the aristocrats who had owned the Bahamas. When granting the land to their ancestors in 1663, Charles II had optimistically declared that the property extended from the Atlantic in the east to the 'South Seas' in the west. By 1718, each of the Carolinas had a governor who presided over a council and an assembly. The council, appointed by London, came to be regarded as officially more important than the locally elected assembly, but in North Carolina things were not always done by the book.

Political rebellions in North Carolina had encouraged a sense of independent self-confidence among the local people. But by 1718 many of the colonists were struggling to get by, having lost livestock and supplies in a violent war with the Native Americans. Their governor, Charles Eden, rarely came under independent scrutiny and like other colonial governors, he was not averse to bending the rules. The Proprietors eventually turned their attention towards the softer South Carolina and few of them ever looked back. Charleston had a good harbour, a better climate and little local opposition to London's way of doing things.

Life was a lot more settled in South Carolina, where councillors like Samuel Wragg bought furs for export to Britain. On 22 May 1718, Wragg, accompanied by his four-year-old son, William, sailed for London aboard the *Crowley*, a ship carrying a cargo that included £1500 in gold and silver coins – equivalent to at least £140,000 today. They had not got far when a well-armed vessel flying a pirate's flag ordered the *Crowley* to heave

A View of Charleston, South Carolina, by Thomas Mellish, eighteenth century.

to. Taking in sail, the frightened crew brought her to a stop and nervously awaited their fate. The pirates quickly boarded and interrogated the passengers before locking them in the depths of the vessel with little light or air.

After bringing his flotilla to the waters off Charleston, Blackbeard had taken up a position beyond a sandbar at the entrance to the port. Capturing every ship that tried to enter or leave the harbour, he effectively held the town to ransom. No pirate had attempted anything quite like this before, certainly not in such a prominent port. Most of the vessels sailing to and from Charleston were twenty to fifty tons, smaller even than Blackbeard's sloop, *Adventure*, which was about eighty tons. But at more than 200 tons, no ship in the harbour matched the sheer size and power of the *Queen Anne's Revenge*. With his flagship and three sloops, Blackbeard commanded a formidable force, boasting up to sixty cannon.

Two pirates were sent ashore. They were accompanied by one of the passengers from the *Crowley*, a man named Marks, who had been given orders to get a medicine chest from the council. He was to warn them that if they refused, the pirates 'would murder all their prisoners, send up their heads to the Governor, and set the ships they had taken on fire'.

After two days, nothing had been heard of the envoys, and Blackbeard's patience was wearing thin. The passengers, led by Wragg, begged for their lives to be spared and the pirates agreed to reprieve them for another twenty-four hours. Before the extra time had passed a small boat with one man aboard came alongside the *Queen Anne's Revenge*. The man told Blackbeard that the envoys' boat had capsized and the men would have drowned had they not been found by fishermen. Marks had paid one of the rescuers to row out to the pirates and tell them what had happened in an attempt to buy more time.

Blackbeard agreed to give the envoys another forty-eight hours – but again, the minutes ticked by with no word from the men on shore. Having now been held captive for five days, the hostages were running out of hope. In desperation they told Blackbeard that if he chose to bombard the town, they would help guide his ships into the harbour, promising to 'stand by [the pirates] to the last man', according to Captain Johnson.

In Charleston, Marks could only guess at the plight of those he had left behind. He had tracked down the governor, Robert Johnson, and given him the pirates' request. In a letter sent less than a month after the siege, the governor wrote despairingly of the 'unspeakable calamity' that had hit the town. His colony was in no position to fight off the pirates: wars with local clans of Native Americans had sapped the treasury, the harbour lay completely unprotected, and there was not a naval vessel within hundreds of miles. The governor and council had no choice but to agree to Blackbeard's demands. While the medicines were prepared, the two pirate envoys swaggered about the streets of Charleston within sight of the furious residents, who 'durst not so much as think of executing their revenge, for fear of bringing more calamities upon themselves'.

Seeking a safe future

Still waiting for news, Blackbeard finally lost patience and coolly sailed his ships into the harbour. With so many guns trained on the vulnerable dockside, panic spread among the people. Any weapons that came to hand were hastily passed around while 'women and children ran about the streets like mad things'. Only when Blackbeard's men were hurriedly sent out to the *Queen Anne's Revenge* with a chest of medicines worth around £400 did their captain call off the blockade and release his hostages.

During the six-day siege he had plundered up to nine ships and kept another eight penned up in the harbour. For a week the pirates had brought Charleston's trade to a halt without firing a shot. During this time Blackbeard stole anything that took his fancy, including goods, valuables and even the clothes of the passengers. But why he demanded nothing more than medicine is a question that cannot be conclusively answered. Up to £1500 was taken from the *Crowley* – which in the American colonies at that time represented a huge amount of money. To put it in context, in 1717 the 2.7 million acres owned by the Crown in Virginia generated a rental income of £1400. Having found gold dust aboard the *Concorde* and money aboard the *Crowley*, by June 1718 the pirates potentially had a combined fortune worth today in the region of a quarter of a million pounds.

Blackbeard now faced a dilemma. To enjoy the benefit of so much cash he would have to spend time on land, like Hornigold, which he could only do after receiving the royal pardon. Yet to go back to the Bahamas might mean having to forfeit both the loot and the lifestyle. Failure to abandon either of these might lead to his execution.

Blackbeard was a man who did not do things by halves; when he wanted a medicine chest he held a port to ransom. Attracted to the free life of a gentleman, he also wanted to continue dabbling in piracy without fear of arrest. Only one place would offer him such freedom: North Carolina. Even there, Blackbeard knew that some things would not be tolerated, such as a flotilla of stolen vessels including a 200-ton ship. The 300 thieves following him in search of easy money also posed a problem, forcing the need for radical action. Thatch secretly came up with a plan that would enable him to get rid of them while keeping the lion's share of the loot.

'Thatch took all away with him'

After the siege of Charleston the pirates sailed up the coast, and as they headed north it was suggested, probably by Blackbeard himself, that the *Queen Anne's Revenge* should be careened. Reaching a deserted beach in this part of the world would not be easy: the North Carolina coastline lies behind a labyrinth of shallow inlets, low-lying islands and treacherous sandbanks. Hidden dangers lurked everywhere and the heavy flagship could be easily grounded, as Blackbeard well knew.

Around 10 June 1718, the pirate flotilla arrived at Topsail Inlet, where the *Queen Anne's Revenge* inevitably struck a sandbar, 'as if it had been done ... by accident,' wrote Captain Johnson. With this action Blackbeard set his treacherous plan in motion. He still had three sloops: the *Adventure*, the Cuban vessel and the *Revenge*, the latter commanded by Lieutenant Richards, who the day before had failed to sink a Boston slave-ship. Blackbeard blamed Richards 'for not burning said Vessel', and he appears to have been consequently excluded from the captain's secret intentions.

Thatch did not even appear to trust the experienced commander of the *Adventure*, Israel Hands. Instead, he sent over to the sloop his wily old quartermaster, William Howard, with a set of specific instructions. While sailing towards his stricken captain in an apparent attempt to pull the ship free, Howard grounded the *Adventure*, so that just a short distance from land the pirates lost two of their four vessels. Since the *Revenge* and Blackbeard's Spanish sloop were too small to accommodate everyone, many men were sent ashore to make their own way up the coast.

Moving to the next part of his plan, Blackbeard suggested that Major Bonnet should find the governor of North Carolina and claim a royal pardon. He promised that on his return the major would be restored to command of the *Revenge*. Bonnet could not have asked for more. Once pardoned, he intended to reunite his old crew and take a privateering commission, financed by his share of the loot.

Bonnet and a handful of his former crew rowed to Bath, a tiny town on the Pamlico River, fifty miles inland. The rest of his men remained in Topsail Inlet. But as they began to prepare the *Revenge* for a privateering voyage against the Spanish, they were overpowered by Blackbeard's own crew, who set about ransacking the *Revenge*. Similar to his actions outside Charleston, Thatch tried to get what he wanted through an elaborate mix of intimidation and treachery rather than cold-blooded violence. Boarding the Spanish sloop, Blackbeard planned to sail north, taking with him a few men and as much of the loot as he could grab. One of the men left behind, Ignatius Pell, later said that 'before they came to any Share of what was taken by Thatch, Thatch took all away with him'.

Those not included in Blackbeard's plan suddenly realized what was going on. In the words of David Herriot, the former captain of the *Adventure*, 'Twas generally believed ... Thatch run his Vessel a-ground on purpose to break up the Companies, and to secure what Moneys and Effects he had got for himself and such other of them as he had most Value for'.

To be sure of grounding the *Queen Anne's Revenge*, Blackbeard may even have recruited a local pilot: members of the crew later remembered seeing a stranger aboard who 'no man could give an account of' and who 'disappeared a little before they were cast away'. 'They verily believed it was the Devil,' wrote Johnson. They were not far wrong.

Blackbeard had no interest in Herriot's protests, and marooned him along with 16 other people on a small, sandy bank, three miles from the mainland. Leaving the crew of the *Revenge* to their fate, Blackbeard sailed out of Topsail Inlet before Bonnet returned. He took with him just forty white sailors and sixty black men, having stolen the flotilla's loot apparently without bloodshed.

Bonnet's naïvety had cost him his ill-gotten gains. He had planned to sail to the Caribbean upon a new-found wave of confidence, but after retrieving his stranded men he abandoned his plans and instead went looking for Blackbeard. A local cider trader who had ferried some of the pirates to shore reported that Thatch had sailed to the small island of Ocracoke; but fortunately for the major, he never saw Blackbeard again.

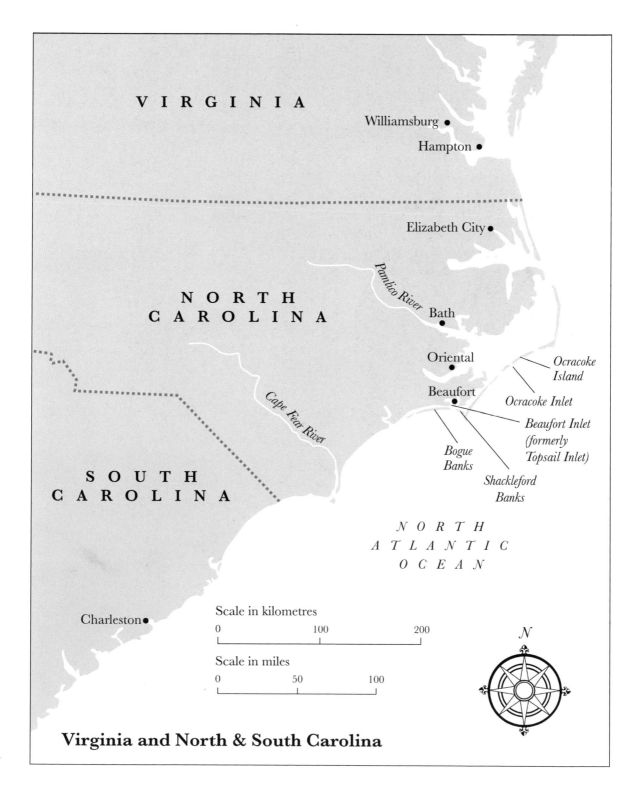

VIRGINIA

Williamsburg ●

Hampton ●

Elizabeth City ●

NORTH
CAROLINA

Pamlico River

Bath ●

Oriental ●

*Ocracoke
Island*

Beaufort ●

Ocracoke Inlet

Cape Fear River

*Beaufort Inlet
(formerly
Topsail Inlet)*

*Bogue
Banks*

*Shackleford
Banks*

SOUTH
CAROLINA

NORTH
ATLANTIC
OCEAN

Scale in kilometres

0   100   200

Charleston●

Scale in miles

0   50   100

N

Virginia and North & South Carolina

Pirate Pastimes

Pirate crews were relatively large, and since many hands made light work, there were long stretches of time aboard a ship when a man had nothing to do. A favourite vice was gambling with cards or dice, which was particularly popular among the buccaneers. One member of John Johnson's crew won 680 silver dollars out of a total prize haul of 800 while playing dice with his shipmates. The jealousy that this kind of thing could cause prompted pirate captains to regulate gambling among their crew. Bartholomew Roberts tried to ban 'gaming' for money altogether, though probably with mixed results.

A safer pastime was music. There were two musicians among Roberts's crew, who, according to the ship's articles, probably did not have much time to themselves: 'The musicians

Wine, women and song: Blackbeard relaxing in a tavern. Still from the television film.

to have rest on the Sabbath Day, but the other six days and nights, none without special favour.' On one occasion, when the rest of the crew were forced to devise their own entertainment, their talents restricted them to a drinking-binge and singing 'Spanish and French songs out of a Dutch Prayer Book'. Many seamen amused themselves with exotic pets such as monkeys and parrots, which could be sold for a high price in Europe. In September 1717, David Randall was selling in London 'Parrokeets which talk English, Dutch, French and Spanish, Whistle at command … very tame and pretty'. A popular vice among all seamen of the age was smoking tobacco (from a clay pipe), which helped to keep hunger and thirst at bay. But one activity was always more popular than anything else aboard pirate ships: drinking.

Dangerous pastimes: *Morgan le Filbustier*, a later engraving by Catel (after Dabelle) from *P. Christian Histoire des Pirates*, 1852

A Carpenter for a Surgeon

Fighting and executions aside, the biggest killers of seamen remained disease and accident. When detailed figures were kept during the Napoleonic era, it was recorded that shipwreck and fire killed 13,000 men, while 70,000–80,000 men died from accident or illness (as noted by historian Brian Lavery). Many European sailors serving in the Indies fell victim to typhus, malaria, dysentery and yellow fever. Popular opinion suggested disease was connected to 'bad air', though some illnesses were better understood than others. Seamen knew effective treatments for scurvy long before James Lind experimentally suggested the use of orange or lemon juice in 1747. But for every man who recommended a diet of fresh fruit and vegetables, five others suggested wonder potions made of assorted ingredients, and seamen found it hard to know whom to believe.

In 1721 the crew of the warship *Weymouth* were delayed by disease in the hunt for pirates off the coast of West Africa. Surgeon John Atkins noted that the ship left England with 240 men and had 'at the end of the Voyage 280 dead upon her Books'. From 1726 to 1728 a Royal Navy squadron in the West Indies commanded by Admiral Hosier lost more than 4000 of its 4750 men to yellow fever, including Hosier himself. It is perhaps no surprise that less than six months after Blackbeard packed a disease-ridden slave-ship with more than a hundred men he urgently needed medicine.

It has been suggested that his crew suffered from syphilis, first encountered by Europeans in the late fifteenth century. The maritime historian N. A. M. Roger found that the incidence of sexually transmitted diseases aboard a group of thirty-three Royal Navy ships during the eighteenth century averaged at around eight per cent per year. This relatively low figure suggests that syphilis, which is not an acute illness like yellow fever, did not have a serious impact upon crews of the period.

While working aboard their small, crowded sailing vessels, seamen spent hours hauling on ropes and dragging heavy stores. Hernias, which were difficult to treat, were a common injury, as were burns and fractures. Pirates in particular could expect to encounter hand-to-

hand fighting, which brought with it the risk of crippling injury. Fighting on cramped decks littered with hand-tools and other iron hardware was a ruthless business that involved anyone in the immediate area. When a member of Captain Low's crew swung at a prisoner with his cutlass, he missed and slashed Low across the face. The ship's surgeon was drunk, and when Low angrily complained about his stitching skills the surgeon punched his captain, telling him to 'sew up his chops himself and be damned'. The pirate code called for quarrels to be resolved on land where things could be more easily controlled.

Bandages were improvised from old cloth, nothing was sterilized, and for a patient awaiting surgery no anaesthetic was available. Alcohol used for this purpose was neither quick nor reliable. Not all surgeons had the correct curved knives, and not all patients had a surgeon. When a member of John Phillips's crew needed his leg amputated, Thomas Fern, the ship's carpenter, carried out the operation. Fern's surgical ability was such that he removed the leg 'in as little time as he could have cut a deal board in two', wrote Johnson. In cauterizing the wound he optimistically tried to use a hot axe, which prevented him working with as 'much art as he performed the other part'.

A man having his leg amputated at sea, *c.* 1820.

The Man From Hell

On reaching the island of Ocracoke, it is possible that the pirates held a council to discuss what to do next. Some made their own way north to Virginia while others, led by Blackbeard himself, went by small boat up the Pamlico River, as Major Bonnet had done, in search of the governor of North Carolina. Arriving at the isolated town of Bath, they found a small collection of buildings nestling close to what was at the time the western frontier.

Located on an inland peninsula amid creeks and rivers, Bath was founded in 1706 by a small number of settlers with grand ideas for the future. Local Native Americans were captured with the intention that slave labour could be used to develop the town and its surrounding plantations. However, the Native Americans themselves did not share this dream. On 22 September 1711, 500 painted warriors, many from the Tuscarora tribe, massacred around 130 settlers in the first of several outbreaks of violence. A peace treaty was signed in 1715, but three years later the inhabitants of Bath were still in no position to fight a band of pirates.

In 1718 North Carolina had no recognized capital and the governor, Charles Eden and his political colleagues, carried out their work in private homes, mainly in and around Bath. Born in 1673 into a titled family from County Durham, Eden had taken up his post in 1714 and lived on a 400-acre plantation on the west side of Bath Creek. Following the treaty with the Tuscarora, the town had experienced a minor boom, but the surrounding countryside, Bath County, remained devastated by the hostilities. Confronted by the possibility of further bloodshed, Eden may have decided that since he could not prevent pirates living in Bath, he should accept their presence as they might be of some use if the Tuscarora were to launch another wave of violence.

Wealthy men visiting such a place would never be entirely unwelcome, whoever they were. All colonial governors were in a position to benefit personally from their posts, and it has long been believed that Eden was one of those who exploited this more than others. He gave certificates of pardon to Blackbeard and around twenty of his men, acting with the support of the colony's chief justice, Tobias Knight. Knight, who also doubled as the secretary of North Carolina, happened to be Eden's neighbour, and between them the two friends wielded considerable power.

Thatch's pardon was issued on dubious grounds. The amnesty only applied to acts of plunder committed before 5 January 1718, yet it later emerged that he and his crew had captured at least twelve ships after this date. His deceit did not stop there. When Thatch arrived in Bath, it is possible that he brought with him the papers from Herriot's *Adventure*. The colony's Vice-Admiralty Court recognized him as the owner of a sloop of this name, and consequently the once anonymous Spanish vessel moored off Ocracoke officially became the *Adventure*. Protected by Eden and Knight, Thatch lived free from fear of arrest and had a sloop that he could legally use.

The man behind the beard

All he lacked was a public label of respectability, and it may have been with this in mind that (so tradition has it) he married Mary Ormond, the sixteen-year-old daughter of a local planter. Supposedly his fourteenth wife, maybe marriage to Mary cemented Blackbeard's position among his newfound friends. The ceremony was said to have been carried out by Eden himself.

So much for the public façade, but what really lay beneath the 'Blackbeard' persona at this point? Some pardoned pirates, like Hornigold and Jennings, proved in later life that they truly

Pirates clearing
the decks of an
East Indiaman,
from a
nineteenth-
century
engraving.

wanted a break from the past. Thatch was a different kind of man. While in North Carolina he robbed local boats and coastal vessels and remained to the end the violent thief he had long shown himself to be.

In his 1974 biography, *Blackbeard the Pirate, A Reappraisal of His Life and Times*, Robert E. Lee suggests that the people of North Carolina considered piracy as a 'fashionable vice', regarding Thatch as a 'celebrity' and his crew as no more than 'lavish scoundrels who … gave with hands as open as when they took'. Captain Charles Johnson also wrote of Blackbeard's apparent popularity, but questioned whether this was 'out of love or fear'. Johnson, in fact, is one of the few writers who saw Blackbeard for what he was: he noted that after marrying Mary, it was Thatch's 'custom to invite five or six of his brutal companions to come ashore, and he would force her to prostitute herself to them all, one after another, before his face'. Maybe some of the politicians found little cause for complaint but local people suffered under the pirates' lawlessness.

Blackbeard spent his days in Bath with the governor and other men involved in the bureaucratic intricacies of the colony, and visited honest planters and their families. Living miles from the sea, they must have had as much interest in maritime matters as he had in them. Thatch created a new lifestyle for himself, shaped by small-town people whose business was agriculture. He lasted a month. In August 1718, Blackbeard returned to sea.

Sailing south towards Bermuda, he encountered two French ships en route home from Martinique, one laden with sugar and cocoa. Thatch captured them on 22 August and, putting the crew of the laden vessel into the empty ship, he took the prize and its cargo back to his hideout at Ocracoke. It is possible that the French crew fought hard to protect their property: after Blackbeard brought the vessel back to the island he would 'suffer no man to go on board except a Doctor to cure his wounded men', according to a newspaper report published in November 1718.

In order to keep his stolen cargo, Thatch knew he needed to give a convincing story to Tobias Knight, the chief justice. At midnight on 14 September, he and four of his men rowed to Knight's waterside home. They took with them gifts of cocoa and sugar in the hope of persuading him that the heavily laden French ship moored down-river had been discovered by chance, without men or papers. After innocently explaining his honest good fortune Blackbeard returned to Ocracoke – and on the way could not help plundering money and brandy from a boat belonging to a local man, William Bell. Bell later swore that when he asked the thief who he was and where he came from, the man replied 'from Hell'. Bell reported the incident to Knight a few hours later, but the chief justice made no mention of whom he might have suspected.

The Vice-Admiralty Court – presided over by Eden and Knight – accepted Blackbeard's story of the abandoned ship, and sixty casks of sugar were awarded to Eden and twenty to Knight. Blackbeard was allowed to keep the rest. It was a watertight explanation and no one could counter his claims, and just in case, he had the ship burnt. Thatch proved he could have it all. Living under the protection of the governor, he could live as he pleased on land, do as he wished at sea, and bring his plunder home with him; even when he robbed the locals, there was little anyone was prepared to do about it. The closest Eden came to condemning him was to tell his council that some 'disorders' had been committed by Thatch's men.

Trouble in Virginia

Before long, however, news of Blackbeard's antics reached a man of a different calibre: the governor of Virginia, Colonel Alexander Spotswood. Spotswood is one of the most intriguing characters in the story of Blackbeard, and other than the pirate captain himself, perhaps the most complicated. A brave, battle-hardened opportunist, he was clear-minded and focused to the point of obsession, and consequently usually got what he wanted. At the same time he was an autocrat whose tenacious style did little to soothe the quarrels that constantly revolved around him. His lengthy, self-congratulatory letters to London, detailing his squabbles with fractious rivals, hum with energy and drive. They also expose him as an abrasive man who left political rivals spinning in his wake.

Alexander Spotswood,
Governor of Virginia,
by Charles Bridges,
eighteenth century.

Spotswood was born in Tangier, North Africa, in 1676, the son of an army doctor belonging to a prominent Scottish family. At seventeen he joined an infantry regiment, later serving under the Duke of Marlborough at the Battle of Blenheim, where he was seriously wounded. When the Earl of Orkney was appointed Governor of Virginia, a royal province since 1624, he appointed Spotswood as his deputy. But – in an arrangement accepted as standard practice – Orkney did not directly govern Virginia himself, and when Spotswood arrived in June 1710, he was given free rein to run the colony.

Spotswood was one of the first governors in the American colonies to appreciate the economic value of the western frontier, and his attempts to improve the welfare of the people of Virginia brought him a degree of popularity. However, some of his measures brought strong criticism, such as the inspection of all tobacco intended for export and the regulation of trade with the Native Americans, and by the spring of 1718 he was in an isolated position. While Blackbeard was holding Charleston to ransom, Spotswood threw a party to mark the king's birthday, in an attempt to heal a rift with eight of the twelve members of his own council. Not even they could snub the king. But instead of attending, the councillors decided to give their own party, leaving the governor feeling 'slighted' by their decision to invite 'all ye Mobb to a Bonfire'.

Putting aside these difficulties, Spotswood threw himself into his work, turning his attention towards pirates. Following the events at Topsail Inlet, so many dubious characters were making their way into Virginia that on 10 July he issued a proclamation requiring all former pirates to make themselves known to the authorities, 'lest they should Seize upon some Vessel'. Among the first men to fall foul of the crackdown was Blackbeard's former quartermaster, William Howard. 'His insolence became so intolerable' wrote Spotswood, that Howard was sent aboard a Royal Navy warship, where he was interrogated about his former voyages.

In the first half of November Howard was committed to trial. He would have to prove he was innocent of piracy or else face the fatal consequences. However, for him the future did not look promising: he paid his lawyer with gold dust. Howard was 'condemned to be hanged, and hung up in Chains'; but the night before his execution, a ship brought news that the king's pardon had been extended to include crimes of piracy committed before 1 July 1718 – and since Howard was not

The docks at Virginia, eighteenth century. A cartouche from *A Map of the Most Inhabited Part of Virginia … drawn by Joshua Fry and Peter Jefferson, 1775.*

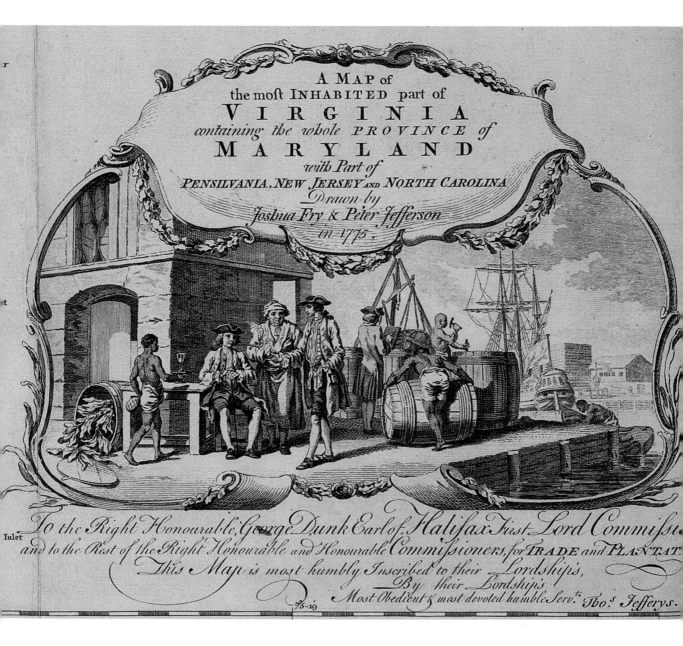

convicted of taking part in any theft after June, he was released. For Spotswood, however, this was a minor annoyance; what mattered was that he had already got from Howard, (and others), all the information he needed about Blackbeard's whereabouts.

A plan to destroy Blackbeard

Putting an end to the exploits of a legendary pirate would be a political coup that not even Spotswood's disgruntled councillors could ignore. Knowing that Blackbeard was within his grasp, Spotswood felt he had to find him, notwithstanding the fact that North Carolina was beyond his jurisdiction. He 'judged it high time to destroy that crew of villains' and embarked on a plan to kill or capture Blackbeard. Spotswood worked in almost total secrecy, keeping his intentions even from his own council, 'there being in this country … an unaccountable inclination to favour pyrates'. First, he needed to gather details of Blackbeard's precise movements and strength without alerting either him or his powerful friends.

The only men with local knowledge of North Carolina whom Spotswood could trust were two of Eden's political enemies, Edward Moseley, a prominent lawyer, and Colonel Maurice Moore, an experienced soldier. Their information, when added to the story told by Howard, gave Spotswood a complete picture of Blackbeard's movements, which he shared with Captain Ellis Brand, commander of one of the two Royal Navy warships stationed in Chesapeake Bay. Brand confidently told the Admiralty in London that he would do all he could to find the pirates and 'if it is possible for me to destroy them … I shall not fail of doing my endeavour'.

It appeared that Blackbeard was dividing his time between Bath and Ocracoke. Bath could be reached either by water or by land, but Ocracoke, fifty miles away, is a small island surrounded by shifting shoals that restrict access to all but the lightest sailing vessels. Virginia's two warships, the *Pearl* and the *Lyme*, were both much bigger than Thatch's *Adventure* and could not operate in shallow or difficult waters.

Next page: Repairing ships in Gosport, Virginia, by George Tobin, 1795, showing a range of vessels that would have been familiar to Blackbeard.

Spotswood needed a plan that could guarantee the capture of Blackbeard wherever he happened to be.

In fact, in the early autumn of 1718 Thatch was spending most of his time on his sloop off Ocracoke, with apparently no clear intention of what to do next. With powerful enemies gathering to the north, it was a dangerous time to start running out of ideas. Already a self-destructive boredom had set in.

One evening Blackbeard was sitting at dinner aboard the sloop with three of his men, including Israel Hands. Beneath the table the captain was clutching two pistols which he suddenly fired indiscriminately without warning. One ball tore through Hands's knee, maiming him for life. According to Captain Johnson, Blackbeard said of his crew 'that if he did not now and then kill one of them, they would forget who he was'. But the incident showed less about discipline than about Blackbeard's brazen disregard for the future, which was soon to prove his undoing.

The 'insolent' William Howard. Still from *Blackbeard: The Real Pirate of the Caribbean*.

Galleons and Gold

Pirates were primarily motivated by the search for loot in the belief that wealth might buy them the freedom to do as they wished. Valuables found aboard a captured vessel were divided into shares and handed out according to a man's rank. Various individuals were awarded a bonus; for example, the crew of Howell Davis agreed that 'he who first espies a sail, if she proves a prize, is entitled to the best pair of pistols on board'.

Everybody received at least one share. Quartermasters, boatswains, gunners, surgeons and carpenters were given around one and a quarter shares each. The master received one and a half shares, and the captain two or more, 'so if the Cheif have a Supream Share beyond his Comrades, 'tis because he's always the Leading Man in e'ry daring Enterprize', wrote 'Barnaby Slush'.

Some money was kept back and given as compensation to anyone wounded in action or injured in an accident. A man could expect to receive up to 800 pieces of eight for the loss of a right arm, down to 100 for the loss of a finger. Maimed seamen often stayed with their ship, like Robert Louis Stevenson's one-legged Long John Silver, who, unable to climb the rigging or join a boarding party, became a sea cook.

While pirates were attracted to easy money and fast living, in practice, the money never came quite as easily as they hoped. Few ships carried a valuable cargo and the average pirate rarely got more than free alcohol and a few pieces of eight. There was no endless supply of gold coins, and those a pirate came across were quickly spent on wine and women. 'They have been known to spend 2 or 3,000 pieces of eight in one night; and one gave a strumpet 500 to see her naked,' wrote Charles Leslie in 1740.

Sea robbers did not have savings accounts, treasure was rarely buried, and maps where X marks the spot are, sadly, fictional. At first glance it seems that a life of freedom lay beyond even the reach of pirates. Although, 300 years later, treasure-hunters are still digging for the fabled piles of gold, little has been found for the simple reason that pirates squandered their cash on 'plenty … pleasure and ease'. It was said of Joseph Mansfield, at his trial in 1722, that drunkenness 'had a great share in drawing him into such company, the love of drink and a lazy life having been stronger motives with him than gold'.

Surrounded by like-minded companions, pirates lived in a form of free democracy that even provided something approaching health insurance. And while soaking up the Caribbean climate, many did indeed find what they had been looking for: a taste of freedom. Galleons and gold might come soon but while they waited, men drank in the sunshine.

Pirate Discipline

In the merchant service, the role of quartermaster, who distributed food and other supplies, was a relatively lowly position; on a pirate ship, however, he was seen as the voice of the men. He held some responsibility for discipline, particularly 'small offences, which are not provided for by the articles', according to Johnson. A quartermaster such as William Howard, who served aboard the *Queen Anne's Revenge*, was elected by the crew and regarded as 'trustee for the whole'.

Jurors who were chosen from among the men and overseen by either the quartermaster or the boatswain dealt with severe breaches of discipline. Traditional punishments aboard any ship included flogging, after which the victim was doused with seawater, salt being the only available antiseptic. A man's ears could be cut off for stealing and a serious offender might be made 'governor of an island' – marooned on a deserted beach with only a pistol and a bottle of water. A man who killed a prisoner who had already freely surrendered could be shot or even lashed to the body of his victim and thrown overboard. Death was also the penalty for desertion and rape.

With so many pirates cramped aboard a small ship, their captain had to be strong-willed and 'pistol-proof'. Days without wind or a shortage of prey could quickly lead to trouble. In his log, Blackbeard wrote: 'Such a Day, Rum all out: – Our Company somewhat sober: – A Damned Confusion amongst us! Rogues a plotting: – great Talk of Separation – So I looked sharp for a Prize: – Such a Day took one, with a great deal of Liquor on Board, so kept the Company hot, damned hot; then all Things went well again'. When chasing, fighting or fleeing from other ships, the captain's word was final. At all other times the crew had a say, as Edward England discovered. Although he would have been content with 'moderate plunder', England 'was generally overruled … and obliged to be a partner in all their vile actions'.

The sense of equality found on a pirate ship broke down any barriers between the senior men and the rest of the crew. Sometimes this was represented literally when the pirates took over a new vessel and pulled down the officers' cabins, making 'the ship flush fore and aft'. Everyone had access to all parts of the ship, with each man sleeping wherever he could find a space, so that even the 'Captain cannot keep his Cabbin to himself'. A successful man like Blackbeard, who captured many ships, might have taken more liberties than other pirate leaders. He liked drinking with his men and it is easy to imagine his cabin resembling a permanent party. At the same time, when he wanted the cabin to himself, how many of his men would dare refuse him?

Capt. EDWARD ENGLAND

Capt. Edward England. Engraving after J. Nicholls, eighteenth century.

CHAPTER

The Hunt for Charles Vane

While Blackbeard was struggling with life on land in North Carolina, radical changes were about to take place in the Bahamas. On the evening of 25 July 1718, a heavily armed ship flying the Royal Navy ensign approached the pirate sloops anchored in the harbour at Nassau. She was the *Rose,* one of three men-of-war accompanying the island's new governor, who himself was aboard a fourth vessel, the *Delicia.* After a voyage of three and a half months, Woodes Rogers had arrived to take up his new post, having been ordered to do all he could to bring pirates to justice.

The *Rose* had got ahead of the rest of the flotilla, and its sudden appearance was too much for one of the pirate captains, Charles Vane. That night he set fire to a captured French vessel and drove her towards the anchored warship. As burning timbers lit up the night sky, showers of sparks rained onto the *Rose,* forcing her crew to cut their cable and sail clear of the harbour.

The following morning Vane followed them into the open sea, but the *Delicia* and the warship *Milford* quickly confronted his sloop. As it fled, Vane's ship was 'wearing the black flag, and fir'd guns of defiance', as Rogers later wrote. Eventually the new governor landed on the waterfront, where 300 people, many of them reformed sea robbers, 'readily surrendered'.

Vane's reckless actions were typical of those who at some point in their lives went on the 'piratical account'. Open defiance traditionally characterized pirates' behaviour. Indeed many adopted a swaggering bravado that was as much about power as about freedom. Such attitudes invited an early grave. To men like

The elusive Charles Vane, as portrayed in *Blackbeard: The Real Pirate of the Caribbean.*

Vane – who sent fire ships towards the king's Navy – death was never far away. Hand-to-hand fighting, duels, accidents, disease and executions all took their toll, with the result that pirates had a life expectancy of about three years, which many apparently accepted with an 'easy come, easy go' mentality. 'A merry life and a short one, shall be my motto,' declared Captain Bartholomew Roberts.

The wrong pirate

Woodes Rogers was determined to capture Vane, but soon after his arrival, he and his men suffered a debilitating illness, blamed by the local people on 'a number of raw hides ... wch. putrified the air'. Rogers was ill for three months, and during this time lost more than eighty of the workers, administrators and settlers he had brought with him. Yet throughout his poor health he did all he could to strengthen his position in Nassau. Rogers quickly formed a council, appointing local people including Thomas Walker, the settler Hornigold had threatened to shoot two years earlier. Hornigold himself, now a reformed man, was given a special task: the capture of Vane.

Charles Vane, who had participated in Jennings's 1716 raid on the Spanish treasure stores in Florida, was not a man to take lightly. His brutality is illustrated in reports written by some of the seamen he captured. On 14 April 1718, he seized the sloop *William and Martha,* whose captain, Edward North, later wrote: 'One of the company they bound hands and feet and ty'd down to the bowspritt with matches to his eyes burning and a pistol loaded with the muzzle into his mouth, thereby to oblige him to confess what money was on board.' North's account was matched by similarly barbaric stories told by seamen aboard a second sloop, the *Diamond,* captured by Vane on the same day. That spring he received a certificate of pardon from the captain of the *Phoenix*, but quickly reneged on his promise to surrender, and even recruited three of the *Phoenix*'s men.

After his encounter with Woodes Rogers at Nassau, Vane stayed in the West Indies, capturing ships from the Bahamas to Anguila. On 15 September 1718, Rogers was told that 'three vessels supposed to be Vaine and his prizes were at Green Turtle Key'. Hornigold was given a sloop and instructed to gather information; when he returned, he brought with him a trader who had had contact with the pirate crew. Rogers wrote that 'This Vaine had the impudence to send me word that he ... expects soon to joyne Majr. Bonnet or some other pirate, and then I am to be attack'd by them.' It was a worrying time and he urgently wrote to the governor of Jamaica asking for soldiers.

But Rogers and Hornigold were acting on old information, for by September Vane was seizing vessels in the waters off Charleston. When the port's beleaguered governor heard that a pirate was careening his vessel in Cape Fear River, North Carolina, he gratefully accepted an offer from a Colonel William Rhett to hunt him down. On the day Rogers was warned that Vane was in the Bahamas, Rhett set sail from Charleston. On reaching Cape Fear at the end of September he found a pirate sloop moored beside two prizes. Following a six-hour gun battle in which at least ten of Rhett's men died, he boarded the sloop and discovered not Vane but Major Bonnet. The major surrendered and was taken back to Charleston, 'to the great joy of the whole province of Carolina'.

After Bonnet had been abandoned in Topsail Inlet in June, he had spent four days hunting for Blackbeard, without success. Accompanied by David Herriot and many members of his original crew, he 'recommenced a down-right pirate, by taking and plundering all the vessels he met with'. Bonnet seized a total of thirteen boats, but by August his sloop *Revenge* was leaking and needed a refit. He found shelter in Cape Fear River, where he remained until Colonel Rhett discovered him in September.

In Charleston, Bonnet was put under guard at a private house, along with Herriot and a third man. All three were interrogated and the deposition provided by Herriot remains one of the most valuable primary sources in the story of Blackbeard. Then, on 24 October, to the great horror of Charleston's citizens, both Bonnet and Herriot escaped. Rumours quickly spread that they were planning a dreadful revenge. The two men fled to an island near the harbour, but a £700 reward offered by South Carolina's governor loosened tongues, and Colonel Rhett soon learnt where they were hiding. For Major Bonnet, for Charles Vane and for Blackbeard, the next few days were to change everything.

Pirate Food and Drink

Food greatly varied aboard fishing boats, merchant vessels and Navy ships, but few crews ate better than pirates. The first of the articles drawn up by pirate captain Bartholomew Roberts declared that 'Every Man has ... equal Title to the fresh Provisions, or strong Liquors, at any Time seized, & use them at pleasure ...'. Pirates plundered whatever they wanted: sometimes they found treasure, but more usually they simply took food, including livestock. More than twenty animal bones, many from cows and pigs, have been found on the wreck of a vessel commanded by Edward Thatch. Ships also carried scores of barrels containing fresh water, salted pork and beef, salted fish, cheese, butter, rum, peas, rice and rock-hard biscuits.

There was plenty of fresh food in the bountiful islands and waters of the Caribbean,

including oranges, lemons, limes and coconuts as well as catfish, grouper and shark. Roberts liked to eat salmagundi, a spicy stew made with pickled herrings; another favourite among pirates was green turtle, which 'eats much like choice veal'. Captain Johnson refers to turtle soup laced with sherry. There are dozens of references to men mixing their drinks, whether they were dipping into the punch bowl or knocking back 'flip', a mixture of beer, rum and sugar. Drinking aboard ship was a dangerous business. In an encounter with Spanish vessels off Peru, Howell Davis's men were so drunk that they failed in twenty attempts to come alongside their prey. Sam Bellamy's loss of the *Whydah* occurred after his men had 'regaled themselves liberally with Madera'.

Above: The Cook's Mate, by Thomas Rowlandson, *c.* 1780.
Left: Bartholomew Roberts's men carousing at Old Calabar River, West Africa.

Devils Incarnate

Pirates had always toyed with death, advertising it on their flags, using it as sport by tormenting their victims and freely relying on it as a punishment. They cared little for the consequences. Having declared war against the world, sea robbers believed they had a right to do as they wished. With oaths to the devil and damnation, pirates flaunted their fearlessness of this world and the next as well. When the *Samuel* was captured by Bartholomew Roberts's crew off the coast of Newfoundland in 1720, her commander, Captain Cary, overheard them declare they would never be hanged: 'For if … they should be Attacked … they would immediately put fire with one of their Pistols to their Powder, and all go merrily to Hell together.'

There was little room in any of this for God. Marcus Rediker has suggested that most seamen had a disregard for religious belief, stemming from practical reality. To get where they were going without drowning on the way, sailors were forced to endure tough, continuous work, which left little time for religion. During a storm, passengers aboard a ship might look to the heavens and pray for salvation, while up above them seamen risked their lives to bring in sail. When heavy seas threatened their ship, sailors struggled to do what they could and only when they could do more did they give religion the benefit of the doubt. 'If they have stopped swearing and started praying there is no hope for us,' one captain told a priest who was travelling as a passenger.

Pirates' tendency to swear and their outrageous behaviour, together with their disregard for the consequences, led many in authority to describe them as devils. Philip Ashton, taken prisoner by Edward Low's crew, considered them 'Devils Incarnate'. Some pirates encouraged this impression, none more so than Blackbeard, who 'stuck lighted matches under his hat' to create an image of something Satanic, just in case his violent behaviour did not make the point well enough. Johnson described an attempt by Blackbeard, and some of his men, to 'make a hell of our own' by sealing themselves in the hold and filling it with burning sulphur until they almost suffocated. 'At length he opened the hatches, not a little pleased that he held out the longest.'

Occasionally priests tried to change seamen's rough ways. En route to New York in 1725, Reverend Ogilvie began to distribute Bibles until members of the crew 'several times attempted to commit Sodomy with him', as the Bishop of London was later informed. Cotton Mather, a minister who presided over executions in Boston, believed that sea robbers 'bid intolerable Defiances to Heaven in their Blasphemies' since each of them 'Mocks at fear'. Members of Roberts's crew may well have agreed. When one was overheard praying to heaven, another asked him, 'Did you ever hear of any Pyrates going thither? Give me Hell, it's a merrier place.'

The 'Devil Incarnate': Blackbeard. Still from the television film.

Toying with death: Blackbeard's emblem struck fear into those who saw it. From *Blackbeard: The Real Pirate of the Caribbean*.

9

CHAPTER

The Battle of Ocracoke

In late September 1718, the most dangerous pirate from the Bahamas to the Carolinas was approaching Ocracoke Island. Now that most of his rivals, including Blackbeard, had officially surrendered, Charles Vane was considered to be the region's greatest threat to shipping. From the deck of a 12-gun brigantine manned by ninety men, Vane fired a salute when he saw Blackbeard's small Spanish boat anchored ahead of him. After the compliment had been returned, the two captains and their crews indulged themselves over several days in a wild party on shore that is still re-enacted locally nearly 300 years later.

It is unlikely that Blackbeard and Vane met by chance on such a small island twenty miles from the mainland, and it is possible that they had arranged the rendezvous after a chance encounter at sea somewhere between Charleston and Bermuda. No doubt their conversation was dominated by events in Nassau. In the past they had each used the port as a base, but the arrival of Woodes Rogers had brought those days to an end. Vane must have recounted with pleasure the moment he drove a fire ship against the *Rose*. Since then he had threatened to attack Rogers with the support of a fellow pirate. Maybe Vane and Blackbeard plotted the recapture of the town that had played such a crucial part in the history of piracy.

Perhaps instead they realized that they needed a new base and may even have considered using Ocracoke itself. Close to the major shipping lanes, the island belonged to North Carolina, whose governor, Charles Eden, could be relied upon to turn a blind eye. True, it had no deep harbour, but this could be an advantage: the Royal Navy's vessels were too cumbersome to negotiate Ocracoke Inlet's treacherous, shallow waters, where shifting sands and uncharted banks could easily ground anything bigger than a sloop. There appeared to be no better place than Ocracoke for a new pirate rendezvous – at least that was the alarming conclusion reached by Governor Alexander Spotswood of Virginia, which was less than a day's sailing away.

Spotswood's plan of attack

Spotswood devised a two-pronged operation that involved sending an armed force by land to Bath and a raiding party by sea to Ocracoke. For this he relied on the support of the two naval commanders whose ships were stationed in Virginia's James River. Ellis Brand, captain of the *Lyme*, would lead the land force; George Gordon, captain of the *Pearl*, would remain with the ships in Virginia while his first lieutenant, Robert Maynard, led men from both vessels in the Ocracoke raid.

The decision to attack Blackbeard at Ocracoke was a turning point in the Royal Navy's campaign against regional piracy, which so far had been largely ineffective. Of the 124 vessels the Navy had on its books in 1718, just nine were stationed in the Americas, including five in the Caribbean, one at New York, one protecting New England, and two in Virginia. Orders issued in March 1717 urging naval captains in Jamaica, Barbados and the Leeward Islands to 'proceed in quest' of sea robbers met with little response.

Between 1716 and October 1718, up to thirty pirate vessels each captured scores of ships every year, while the Navy failed to destroy a single pirate crew. To Captain Johnson it appeared 'as if one was much more diligent in their affairs than the other'. Pirates' local knowledge allowed them to exploit narrow inlets and shallow waters through the use of small sloops, and in so doing they proved themselves to be simply more capable than the Navy.

Several colonial governors believed the Navy was not doing all that it could. In July 1717 the governor of Barbados warned that 'the King's shipes in America are commonly so much disabled by sickness, death, and desertion of their seamen, that they are often constrain'd to lye near two thirds of the year in harbour'. In 1717, the *Pearl* and the *Lyme* arrived in Virginia, though their crews saw no action until November 1718, when Governor Spotswood took the lead in planning the operation against Blackbeard. Meanwhile, in Nassau, Woodes Rogers begged the Admiralty to place any naval captains sent his way 'under ye direction of ye Goverment and Council ...'.

The naval seamen themselves were less concerned with politics than with evading boredom and disease. They were well disciplined, and the comparative cleanliness and efficiency of their ships contrasted sharply with any pirate vessel. They received regular, hot meals that frequently included meat or fish, together with generous quantities of beer. In terms of supplies they were no worse off than they would have been working ashore, but their arduous conditions and low pay led to a continuous trickle of desertions.

The secret warning

Leaving the naval officers to work out the details of the attack on Blackbeard, Spotswood urged Virginia's assembly to pass an act promising to pay £100 to anyone who either captured or killed Thatch, in the hope that this would stiffen the resolve of the raiding parties. Smaller amounts were offered for Blackbeard's officers and men, 'according to the Quality and Condition of such Pyrates'. Since Spotswood could not allow his plan to be leaked to Thatch's contacts either in Virginia or North Carolina, he refused to explain to his colleagues his sudden interest in granting cash rewards.

When the naval officers realized that the shallow waters around Ocracoke prevented them using their own vessels, they told Spotswood they needed small civilian sloops, which he would have to hire quietly at his own expense. Lieutenant Maynard, described by Captain Johnson as an 'experienced officer and gentleman of great bravery and resolution', was given the *Jane*, while Midshipman Hyde from the *Lyme* was to command a smaller sloop, the *Ranger*. They took fifty-three men from the two men-of-war, along with plenty of small arms, but no cannon, which would weigh the boats down and increase their chance of grounding. Eventually all was ready, and Spotswood's secret operation could begin.

In fact, Spotswood had not managed to keep the plan secret from everyone: Blackbeard had many powerful friends. He was on good terms with both Governor Eden and North Carolina's chief justice, Tobias Knight, who between them had granted him a pardon, sanctioned his use of a stolen sloop, accepted plundered goods and ignored complaints from local people who had been robbed. When Knight learned of Spotswood's plan to capture Thatch, he was not slow to warn him.

In a note urging him to leave Ocracoke, dated 17 November 1718, Knight told Blackbeard: 'If this finds you yet in harbour I would have you make the best of your way up as soon as possible your affairs will let you. I have something more to say to you than at present I can write.' Signing himself 'your real ffriend', Knight sent the letter via three of Thatch's men, insisting they 'bid him be upon his guard'.

But Blackbeard had received other warnings in the past which had proved groundless, and he considered this latest one to be no different. It was a fatal mistake. On the day Knight wrote his letter, the two small sloops under the command of Lieutenant Maynard quietly slipped out of Hampton into Chesapeake Bay, while Captain Brand left Virginia for Bath at the head of another armed force, guided by Edward Moseley and Colonel Maurice Moore.

Lost opportunities

Why did Blackbeard stay at Ocracoke? When visiting these waters in previous years he had sailed south by mid-November in search of warmer weather. He could easily have evaded Spotswood by cruising back towards the shipping lanes off Bermuda, where he had discovered the French merchant ships three months earlier. On 17 November 1717, Blackbeard had captured the *Queen Anne's Revenge* and then embarked on a daring voyage of plunder that took him across the Caribbean. On 17 November a year later, the Navy was looking for him, as he knew from a letter written the day they had left Virginia, yet still he stayed where he was.

Perhaps Blackbeard was clear about his intentions; perhaps he had no plan at all. By late 1718, he had captured and killed his way to the top. He had commanded a flotilla from aboard a 36-gun flagship; he had gold dust and silver plate and enough cash and fine clothes to impress any of his fourteen wives. He had a pardon and access to a colonial governor; he had a sloop and an island hideaway. There was nothing left to look for, except trouble.

Perhaps he had a plan for the future that included an attack on Woodes Rogers alongside Charles Vane, who had left Ocracoke in October after gloating about his moment of glory over the Navy. In the Caribbean, Blackbeard's name was over-shadowed by Vane's – and so, too, in Charleston, where Blackbeard's siege in May had been eclipsed by Vane's robberies in September. Thatch himself had never taken on the Royal Navy. The stories of his attack on the *Scarborough* in late 1717 were for everybody else, for he himself knew them to be false. Equipped with nothing more than a small Spanish boat and a handful of men, he was in no position to fight anything bigger than a sloop.

In November 1718, Blackbeard could either join Vane in an attack on Rogers – under Vane's command – or he could stay where he was, wait for the Navy and prove that he could defy anyone who came after him. Any battle would be fought in familiar waters: he would win or he would die trying.

Thatch had around eighteen men though 'he gave out to all the vessels he spoke with that he had forty', reported Johnson. Among the crew were his boatswain Garrat Gibbens, gunner Phillip Morton, and seamen Thomas Gates, James Blake and Caesar – a man who was described by Johnson as a 'resolute fellow, a Negro whom [Blackbeard] had brought up'. Other men, including Israel Hands, were in Bath rather than on board the *Adventure*, and so not immediately at hand for any action that might take place.

Maynard's crew fires on Blackbeard. From *Blackbeard: The Real Pirate of the Caribbean*

'Damn you for villains! Who are you?'

On the evening of Thursday, 21 November, while Captain Brand's land force was still fifty miles short of Bath, Maynard's sloops dropped anchor on the south-eastern side of Ocracoke. The top of a mast poking above the grassy dunes gave away the pirates' position on the other side of the island. To prevent news of their arrival reaching Blackbeard, all vessels en route to Bath were stopped from entering Ocracoke Inlet, while seamen heading in the opposite direction were asked for information. Despite these precautions Blackbeard soon discovered that the Navy had arrived. He ordered his eight cannon to be loaded, and spent the night drinking with Samuel Odell, the master of a trading sloop.

The following morning, the thirty-three men aboard the *Jane* sailed cautiously into Ocracoke Inlet, accompanied by the *Ranger* and her crew of twenty-two. The sloops were guided by depth-soundings taken from a small boat – which was suddenly spotted by the pirates. Firing pistols, Thatch's men quickly cut their anchor cable and approached the *Jane* head-on until their vessel grounded in the shallows. The *Jane* was too heavy to close in on her target and as Maynard ordered their ballast to be thrown overboard, Blackbeard called out: 'Damn you for villains! Who are you?'

Maynard identified himself and threatened to board the pirates' sloop. Demanding a drink, Blackbeard defiantly cried out: 'Damnation seize my soul if I give you quarter, or take any from you!' Then, at his command, the pirates fired a

Blackbeard and Maynard fight to the death. Still from the television film.

devastating broadside, unleashing a lethal volley of partridge-shot. At such short range the containers carrying hundreds of small iron pellets caused carnage aboard the *Jane*, killing and wounding twenty men. Hyde, the commander of the *Ranger*, was also killed, and there were a further eight casualties among his crew.

Before the pirates had time to fire again, Maynard ordered his men to take shelter in the hold, where they reloaded their pistols and muskets. This decision spared them from an onslaught of 'new-fashioned sort of grenades', described by Johnson as 'case bottles filled with powder and small shot, slugs, and pieces of lead or iron, with a quick match in the mouth of it'. As the *Jane* closed in on the *Adventure*, only Maynard, the helmsman and a pilot, William Butler, stayed on deck. Aboard his sloop Blackbeard could see that it would not be long before the enemy were upon them, and he ordered Caesar to ignite the powder and create a single catastrophic explosion should the Navy get the better of them. As the two boats crunched into one another, the pirate captain saw that the deck of the *Jane* was virtually empty and jubilantly declared that the enemy seamen were all 'knocked on the head'.

Through the smoke from the grenades, Maynard saw the sinister silhouettes of fifteen pirates clamber across the bows of the *Jane*, and urgently called to his men in the hold. Before Blackbeard had time to attack him, around a dozen of the surviving Navy sailors raced on to the deck and ran at Thatch's men 'with as much bravery as ever was done upon such an occasion'. In the mêlée, Blackbeard and Maynard fired pistols at each other before Thatch lunged at the lieutenant with his sword. Around them battered bodies lay upon a deck slippery with blood, as men desperately hacked at each other using any weapon that came to hand.

Slashing at the huge pirate captain, Maynard broke his cutlass on Blackbeard's cartridge box and was forced to step back to hurriedly cock a pistol. It was the chance Thatch had been waiting for. But before he could strike, a Highlander among Maynard's crew hacked at the pirate, giving 'him a terrible wound in the neck and throat'. Maynard later wrote

The aftermath: a blood-spattered Maynard. Still from *Blackbeard*.

that Blackbeard 'fell with five Shot in him, and 20 dismal Cuts in several Parts of his Body'. Beside him eight of his fellow pirates lay dead or dying, while many of the wounded jumped overboard so that 'the sea was tinctured with blood'. They were picked up by the crew of the *Ranger*, who also captured the few pirates still aboard the *Adventure*, together with the unfortunate local trader who had joined them for a drink the night before.

The demonic reputation that Thatch himself had done much to encourage had finally tempted the authorities to hunt him down. But in looking for a scrap with the Navy he underestimated their ability to capture him and found himself in a battle that ultimately claimed his life. Blackbeard's destruction, Johnson wrote, 'was entirely owing to the conduct and bravery of Lieutenant Maynard and his men'. It came at a high price. Of Maynard's fifty-four crewmen, around ten were killed and twenty-three wounded. Nine pirates lay dead, including Blackbeard, Garrat Gibbens and Phillip Morton, and another nine were captured, all of whom were injured.

The pirates' initial broadside that claimed so many sailors may, in the end, have saved the day for the Navy; immediately after it, the *Jane*'s crew, hidden in the hold, appeared to have vanished and their sloop was quickly boarded by Blackbeard. Had Maynard led his men onto the *Adventure*, Caesar might have carried out Blackbeard's final order. Waiting with a lighted match in the magazine, he attempted it but was prevented by Samuel Odell.

Perhaps Blackbeard had underestimated Maynard's determination – or perhaps he had known that a violent death was inevitable, and was ready to take on the Navy come what may. For him, there was honour in dying in battle, a fitting end for a pirate captain of his reputation. Once larger than life, he was now demonized in death. Thatch's head was cut off and tied to the bowsprit of the *Jane*, while his body was thrown over the side. Legend has it that the headless corpse then swam around the battered sloops.

Maynard stayed at Ocracoke for up to three weeks while his wounded men rested. He gathered together the pirates' possessions, and searched their boat and their camp ashore for

Blackbeard's head tied to the bowsprit of the *Jane*. From a nineteenth-century book on pirates.

the fabled hoard of treasure. Johnson wrote that on the night before the battle, one of Thatch's crew asked the captain whether his wife knew where he had buried the money. Blackbeard replied that 'nobody but himself and the devil knew where it was, and the longest liver should take all'.

Pistols and Cutlasses

Unlike the crew of a merchant vessel or warship, pirates were always armed, as indicated by the articles of Captain Phillips, which warned that any man who 'shall not keep his Arms clean, fit for an Engagement ... shall be cut off from his Share ...'. The flintlock small arms of the period were sometimes unreliable and took time to load. Gunpowder was poured into the barrel followed by a lead ball, which was kept in place with wadding. More powder was placed on the pan – part of the gun's firing mechanism. A spring-loaded 'cock' gripped a flint that snapped against a steel frizzen once the trigger was pulled. The resulting spark ignited the powder on the pan, which in turn ignited the charge in the barrel.

Fine handguns were highly prized. Johnson wrote that pirates 'endeavoured to outdo one another in the beauty and richness of their arms, giving sometimes at an auction (at the mast) thirty or forty pounds a pair, for pistols. These were slung in time of service, with different coloured ribbands over their shoulders ...' The articles of George Lowther awarded the man who first spotted a prize the best pistols aboard her. Those without a firearm made do with a cutlass – a short sword with a heavy blade that was not officially phased out by the Royal Navy until 1936.

Other hand-weapons were more indiscriminate. A small pot filled with gunpowder and containing a lighted fuse was in common use by 1700. Nicknamed *granada* ('pomegranate') by the Spanish, such pots came to be known as 'grenades' and were used with devastating effect by pirates, not least Blackbeard.

Pirates' small-arms. *Left:* a nineteenth-century boarding axe, useful in striking through rigging when boarding. *Above:* a walnut and silver pistol belonging to privateer Captain Peter Reed, made in London, *c.* 1730. *Below:* a silver and stag-horn hunting sword of the type commonly used at sea (possibly a forerunner of the cutlass), made in London, 1702

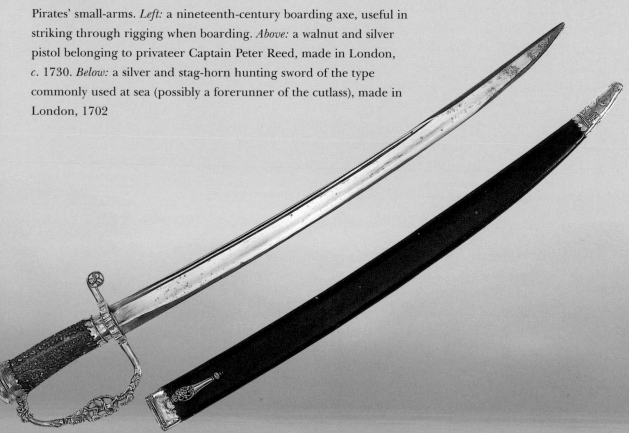

Arrested for Piracy

Legally, a variety of actions were regarded as piracy, such as abusing a privateering commission, or robbing a ship riding at anchor while her men were ashore. The Lord High Admiral (in practice the Admiralty, on behalf of the Crown) claimed jurisdiction over any action taken against any subject of the British monarch anywhere in the world. The robbery did not even have to take place on the high seas: if it occurred below the low-tide mark, it was piracy. Accused men were to be arrested but did not need to be tried. Captain Johnson believed that 'If Pyracy be committed on the Ocean, and the Pyrates in the attempt be overcome, the Captors may, without any Solemnity of Condemnation, hang them up at the Main-Yard.'

Those pirates who were brought to trial faced the death penalty, as did anyone who profited from their actions. 'An Act for the more effectual Suppression of Piracy', originally drafted in 1698 and extended several times afterwards, threatened death to anyone agreeing to 'truck, barter, [or] exchange' with pirates. The act also allowed sailors who failed to defend their ship to be jailed.

After 1700, colonial governors were entitled to preside over piracy trials in local Vice-Admiralty courts. Captured pirates who were brought to London were held in the Marshalsea Prison on the south bank of the Thames to await trial at the Old Bailey. They would have to conduct their own defence in a hearing that would last one or two days and which would almost certainly result in a death sentence.

North View of the Marshalsea, Southwark, before the New Buildings.
Engraving from *The Gentleman's Magazine*, 1803.

10
CHAPTER

Searching for Justice

Blackbeard and his men were not the only pirates in the region for whom time ran out in the autumn of 1718. On 4 November, in Charleston harbour, Richard Worley and twenty-five of his crew were killed in a furious battle with four armed sloops under the command of South Carolina's governor, Robert Johnson; another twenty-four of his men were captured, most of whom were quickly tried and executed. The following day, Major Bonnet was recaptured by Colonel Rhett on a nearby island, while David Herriot was fatally wounded. His death spared him the humiliation of having to watch a judge examine his seven months as a pirate.

Meanwhile, the trial of Bonnet and Herriot's shipmates had already begun in Charleston under Judge Nicholas Trott. By the time Bonnet became the thirty-fourth and last member of his ill-fated crew to be brought before the court, twenty-nine of his men had been hanged at White Point, south of the town.

Bonnet's trial began on Monday 10 November, and in his defence he optimistically claimed that the thirteen vessels robbed by the men under his command were nothing to do with him, 'for I never gave my Consent to any such Actions: For I often told them, if they did not leave off committing such Robberies, I would leave the Sloop'. In his detailed summing up, Judge Trott told him that he had killed eighteen people during the two attempts to bring him into custody. He added that although Bonnet was 'generally esteemed a Man of Letters', the 'Principles of Religion that had been instilled into

Major Stede Bonnet, from the *Histories and Lives of All the Most Notorious Pirates and their Crews*, London, 1725.

you by your Education have been . . . entirely defaced . . . by the Infidelity of this wicked Age . . . '. Trott sentenced Bonnet to death, and despite a pitiful plea for clemency the major was hanged at White Point on 10 December. By the end of the year a total of forty-nine pirates had been hanged in Charleston, while in North Carolina a further twenty-five were either captured or killed – among them Blackbeard. After years of tough talk about exterminating nests of pirates, the authorities were finally fighting back.

Executions and narrow escapes

The news of Blackbeard's death took some time to reach the rest of his pursuers. On 23 November, the day after the battle at Ocracoke, Brand's land force reached Bath and was told that the pirate was expected at 'every minute'. After entering the town, Brand went to Governor Eden's house and informed him that he was hunting for Blackbeard by the authority of the governor of Virginia. He handed Eden a letter in which Spotswood gave his reasons for sending armed men to North Carolina.

With no sign of Blackbeard, Brand sent two canoes down the Pamlico River the following day to discover whether he had been caught. On 26 November they returned with the triumphant news that the pirate captain had been killed, and in mid-December Maynard sailed up to Bath with Blackbeard's head still hanging from his bowsprit. He showed Brand 'several letters and written papers' incriminating the pirates and their friends. Discovered aboard the *Adventure*, they included the warning sent by Tobias Knight to Blackbeard on 17 November.

In January 1719 Brand travelled back to Virginia by land while Maynard returned by sea, taking with him Blackbeard's sloop and sixteen pirates arrested at Ocracoke and Bath. The captured men were charged with piracy, and their trial began in Williamsburg on 12 March. Five admitted everything in the hope of leniency, including Israel Hands. Hands, who had been arrested in Bath, confirmed that the French sugar ship supposedly found abandoned at sea had in fact been captured. Other pirates, including Thomas Gates and James Blake,

Next page: Blackbeard and Israel Hands plotting in the cabin at the peak of their piratical career.

From *Blackbeard: The Real Pirate of the Caribbean.*

described how on 14 September they had taken some of the ship's cargo of cocoa and sugar to the home of Tobias Knight. William Bell, the local boatman who was robbed the same night, recounted his fruitless conversation with Knight.

Samuel Odell, the trader who had been drinking with Blackbeard the night before the Battle of Ocracoke, was the only one of the sixteen to be acquitted. Captain Johnson wrote that Odell received seventy wounds during the fighting, 'notwithstanding which, he lived, and was cured of them all'. Israel Hands, like William Howard, benefited from another extension to the King's pardon. He, too, was released and, according to Johnson, finished his days begging on the streets of London. The remaining fourteen men, including Caesar, Gates and Blake, were executed with little ceremony outside Williamsburg.

'Privy to the Piracys committed by Edward Thache'

As far as Spotswood was concerned, the trial was not only about condemning the captured pirates, but about exposing Charles Eden and Tobias Knight. As Chief Justice, Secretary of the Colony and Collector of Customs, Knight was almost as important as Governor Eden himself. After the trial, the pirates' damning depositions were sent to Eden along with Bell's testimony and other documents, including Knight's letter to Blackbeard. According to officials in Virginia, everything suggested that Knight was 'privy to the Piracys committed by Edward Thache and his Crew, and hath recieved and concealed the Effects by them piratically taken, whereby he is become an accessary'.

Eden had no choice but to put his friend on trial, or else the claims would go unanswered and he would remain tainted by them. Members of the council, including Eden himself, tried Knight in North Carolina on 27 May 1719. Fighting hard to prove his innocence, Knight insisted that the 'pretended Evidence is every word false', and succeeded in sowing enough doubt for his friends to find it easy to acquit him. However, the case weakened his failing health, and he died within a few weeks of the hearing.

Eden himself never faced a trial, despite the efforts of Edward Moseley and Colonel Maurice Moore who, on 26 December 1718, forced their way into the office where the colony's records were kept in search of incriminating documents. Both men were subsequently arrested and their trial for this and other offences dampened further political opposition in North Carolina throughout the remaining years of Eden's life. He died of yellow fever while still in office in 1722. Wars with Native Americans, along with the relative poverty of the colony, prevented Eden from stamping any notable mark on the province and his limited successes have since come to be tarnished by his association with Blackbeard. In later years Moseley went on to become a chief justice and died in 1749, six years after Moore.

On the day that Spotswood heard of Maynard's success at Ocracoke he wasted no time in telling London of his efforts to protect 'the trade of these Plantations', referring not only to Virginia but also to her neighbouring colonies. Spotswood was careful with his choice of words, for he knew he had strayed beyond his jurisdiction by conducting an operation in North Carolina without the knowledge or consent of its authorities. He expressed the hope that 'Success may atone for that Omission', but his opinion was not shared by Eden and his supporters, who justifiably felt that their powerful neighbour had taken advantage of North Carolina's weakness. When they challenged Spotswood's legal right to invade a colony owned by the Lords Proprietors, he was compelled to explain himself.

In a letter to Lord Carteret, one of the Proprietors, Spotswood suggested that since he had succeeded in 'Rescueing the Trade of North Carolina from the Insults of Pyrates', his actions would 'not be unacceptable to Your Lordships'. He admitted that he had not informed either the Proprietors or Eden about the plan, but chose not to mention that this was because he believed Eden to be in cahoots with Blackbeard. Instead, he claimed to have done Eden a great service by excluding him, for had he been 'lett into that Secret' the pirates might have attacked him if Maynard's operation had failed. Besides, as Spotswood indelicately put it, Eden and his friends 'could contribute nothing to the Success of the Design'. Both sides hardened their positions until the question of jurisdiction was lost in a tangled web of legal argument. Ultimately it seemed clear that Spotswood had over-reached himself, but that Eden lacked the power to do much about it.

Cash rewards

Despite the Virginian government's promise to reward those involved in Blackbeard's death 'punctually and justly', nobody received a penny for four years due to a bitter quarrel over the distribution of the cash. The money was finally paid only after Lieutenant Maynard and his men, who had risked their lives at Ocracoke, agreed to share it with their shipmates who had stayed behind aboard the *Pearl* and the *Lyme*. It amounted to a little over £334.

It is not clear what became of Maynard. One story suggests that a few years later he 'suffered a sudden death at the hand of two Negro slaves' in Virginia. Captain Brand returned to England, where in July 1719 he was threatened with prosecution for trespassing upon the territory of the Lords Proprietors. Spotswood sent letters in support of his case and it appears that nothing came of it. Brand remained in the Navy, reaching the rank of rear admiral in 1747.

Spotswood rejoiced in the success of the attack against Blackbeard. But the political difficulties it created contributed to the growing clamour mounting against him, which he never successfully silenced. Spotswood had a habit of over-playing his hand and then using his powerful position to brush aside dissent, but eventually his old tricks caught up with him. On 20 November 1718, Virginia's House of Burgesses listed its arguments against him and one of the colony's disaffected councillors, then in England, was asked to present them to the King. This open ill feeling continually gnawed at Spotswood's position until eventually he was toppled from government on 3 April 1722, 'doubtless the result of an accumulation of grievances'.

In the meantime, he went in fear of his life, telling the Council of Trade and Plantations on 31 May 1721 that he had received word that '[Bartholomew] Roberts, a Pirat ... would make Virginia a Visit and revenge the Death of the Pirats which [have] been executed here'. Spotswood built gun batteries at the mouth of the James River and elsewhere, and urged London to send him stronger warships, insisting that a '... 40 or 50 Gun Ship is absolutely necessary to Convoy our Merchant Ships out to Sea ... ' After deciding to return to Britain in 1724, he wrote another letter to the Council of Trade and Plantations, expressing once again his fear of pirates. He asked '... what inhuman treatment must I expect, should I fall within their power, [I] who have been markt as the principle object of their vengeance ...' and he requested passage on a warship as protection from 'barbarous Wretches' intent on punishing him 'for cutting off their arch Pirate Thatch'.

Once safely back in London, Spotswood married Anne Butler Brayne, and six years later they returned to his extensive and successful business interests in Virginia. He died in 1740. Although he had successfully taken on the most feared pirate captain of the day, Spotswood's bold operation against Blackbeard was overshadowed by divisive political argument. However his twelve years as governor had a lasting impact on Virginia, as noted by the Privy Council, which recorded that he had done 'more than any other person towards peopling the country'.

Like Spotswood, Woodes Rogers also found that his efforts in bringing sea robbers to justice were largely ignored. Despite ensuring that Nassau was never again the infamous pirates' haunt of former days, he was generally forgotten by London and was forced to rely on his own limited resources. His repeated requests for reinforcements went unanswered and, isolated and unsupported, he suffered further ill health. In 1721 he was forced to give up his post, though he returned as governor eight years later. As Cordingly put it, Rogers was 'one of the heroes of the war against pirates', but he wore himself out with his work and died at Nassau on 15 July 1732.

The legend of Blackbeard

After being taken from the bowsprit of the *Jane*, Blackbeard's head was erected on a pole on the west side of the mouth of the Hampton River, where it served as a warning to pirates. In later years it was supposedly turned into the base of a punch-bowl and put on display at the Raleigh Tavern in Williamsburg. It subsequently vanished, and was not heard of until the first half of the twentieth century, when the substantial part of a silver-plated skull turned up in the hands of a private collector. Today this skull is in the collection of the Peabody Essex Museum in Salem, Massachusetts, although its authenticity remains unconfirmed.

Over the last three centuries many fun and fabulous tales have come down to us which, true or not, enrich the enduring story of Blackbeard. He reportedly relaxed at Teach's Oak near Oriental in North Carolina, where modern-day campers have heard screams and seen a 'huge bloody eye'. Blackbeard is said to have lived in 'The Old Brick House' near Elizabeth City, which is described as having a tunnel that leads from the basement to the water's edge and which was built no earlier than 1735. Another tunnel is supposed to have allowed him to bring goods to Eden's mansion from the banks of Bath Creek, but today only the foundations of this building remain. Blackbeard also reputedly lived on the other side of the creek at Plum Point, where there exist more ruined foundations, surrounded by much evidence of digging – a sure sign of treasure-hunters.

Those looking for Blackbeard's chest of plundered gold are said to be guided by a mysterious glow known as 'Teach's light', particularly on winter evenings. However, treasure-hunters, who seem to favour dark, stormy nights when looking for loot, apparently find the pirate's headless ghost more than anything else. According to legend Blackbeard buried his priceless – and endless – treasure in a large number of places, including Money Island near Wilmington, Holiday's Island in the Chowan River, and Blackbeard Island off the Georgia coast.

But is there anything for the fortune-seekers to find? Pirates plundered perishable provisions far more frequently than they stole gold and silver, and Blackbeard was no exception. As well as Thatch's head, Maynard brought back to Virginia twenty-five barrels of sugar, eleven casks and 145 bags of cocoa, a barrel of indigo and a bale of cotton, together with another twenty barrels of sugar and two bags of cotton found by Brand in Tobias Knight's barn.

Everything, including the *Adventure*, was sold at auction for £2238, from which Spotswood deducted 'the Charges of recovering ye s'd Effects out of the hands of the Pyrats, the Transportation from Carolina, [and] the Storage and Expense of the Sale'. According to Robert E. Lee, 'There is no record of the amount, if any, remaining, or of who received the remainder.' Nor is there any record of Spotswood receiving any of Blackbeard's legendary hoard of valuables. Where were the gold and silver, the gemstones and the cash? It seemed that they had never existed after all.

In fact, they were as real as the rumours suggested. While in Bath, Maynard showed Brand some gold dust, silver plate and 'other small things of plunder' that he had found aboard the *Adventure*. The lieutenant later secretly distributed some of the loot amongst those who fought beside him at Ocracoke, keeping nearly half for himself – worth about £90, according to Captain Gordon, commander of the *Pearl*. Though this cost Maynard the support of Spotswood, among others, it guaranteed payment for the great risks he had undertaken – just in case the promise of rewards came more quickly than the fact, as proved to be the case.

Who made the most from Blackbeard's plundered gold? Probably the man who had been brave enough to take him on. Maynard showed there was gold to be made from the pirate crew – perhaps one day more will come to light and he will not be the last to profit from their hoard. It is a thought that has helped to keep Blackbeard's name alive for nearly 300 years.

Looking for Revenge

Occasionally sea robbers referred to a 'brotherhood' of piracy, a self-perception that safeguarded two popular customs. Firstly, pirates never attacked each other; as Blackbeard showed when inviting Vane, his rival, to Ocracoke. Secondly, executed pirates were to be avenged, again as demonstrated by Thatch in attacking the *Great Allen* from Boston, where some of Sam Bellamy's men had been hanged. In 1721, Spotswood was justified in taking seriously Bartholomew Roberts's threats of revenge. Eight months earlier, some of Roberts's men 'openly and in the daytime burnt and destroyed our vessels in the Road of Basseterre [St Kitts]', after pirate executions at Nevis. The governors of both Barbados and Martinique tried to capture Roberts, and in his fury he adorned his flag with an image of himself standing on two skulls above the letters A. B. H. ('A Barbadian's Head') and A. M. H ('A Martinican's Head' – *see* page 83).

The notion of revenge was reflected in the names of at least eight pirate vessels (among them Major Bonnet's *Revenge* and Blackbeard's *Queen Anne's Revenge),* as noted by Marcus Rediker. Although such attitudes sometimes appeared to be no more than a half-hearted attempt to give meaning to their actions, pirates went great lengths in avenging common seamen who had been mistreated by merchant captains. Captured merchant crews were questioned about their commander's conduct, for many captains had a poor record. Captain Skinner of the *Cadogan*, who dumped some of his surplus seamen into the Royal Navy, was later caught by them after they had joined the pirate Edward England. England's men 'pelted him with glass bottles [and] whipped him about the deck, till they were weary', before shooting him in the head.

Merchant seamen suffered a variety of barbaric punishments at the hands of their captains. In 1707 Captain Wherry grabbed hold of James Conroy and, using his thumb, 'wilfully, designedly, & malitiously maimed & put out' his eye. After stealing a chicken, Anthony Comerford was tied to the rigging by Commander John Pinkethman and ordered to receive two lashes from each member of the crew; he died before the punishment was completed. Few ordeals, though, compared with that of Andrew Andrewson, who was beaten 'upon the head with an Elephant's dry'd Pizle'. Moments before he was hanged in 1724, John Archer, who once served with Blackbeard, hoped 'that Masters of Vessels would not use their Men with so much Severity, as many of them do, which exposes us to great Temptations' – not least, piracy.

Victims of Piracy

Seamen who resisted a pirate attack or tried to hide their valuables did so at great risk. After taking the *Greyhound* at the end of an hour-long gun battle in 1722, George Lowther's crew 'whipped, beat, and cut the men in a cruel manner'. When Edward Low heard that the captain of the Portuguese ship *Nostre Signiora de Victoria* had dropped a bag containing 11,000 gold coins into the sea, he 'ordered the captain's lips to be cut off; which he broiled before his face, and afterwards murdered him and all the crew'. Francis Spriggs, 'wanting a little diversion', tied up a group of captured seamen and after hauling them as high as the main top 'let them run down, enough to break all the bones in their skins'. *The Times* of 23 July 1829, included a report of the crew of a Dutch brig who were compelled to 'what is termed "walk the plank"'. Despite lurid scenes in various pirate books and films, the *Times* article refers to one of only two known examples of this practice.

Other victims were forced to run round a mast while being jabbed by anything that came to hand, in a 'game' called 'sweating'. Alternatively, slow-matches might be tied to men's fingers 'which burnt all the flesh off the bones', while 'woolding' (which normally referred to the lashing of masts to strengthen them) involved winding cords around a man's head until his eyes 'burst out of the skull'.

Bartholomew Roberts's crew went further than most, carrying out a horrific act of destruction off the West African coast on 12 January 1722. After Captain Fletcher of the *Porcupine* refused to meet their demands, the pirates decided to burn his ship which lay anchored off the port of Whydah. When they went below they discovered eighty slaves and started to cut their chains, but gave up when they found that 'unshackling them cost much time and labour'. Leaving the slaves where they were, the pirates set the ship alight and then fled. The men and women who had been released jumped overboard – only to be attacked by sharks.

Examples of the pirate code specified execution as the mandatory penalty for rape, but despite this Captain Johnson documents several disturbing cases of women captured at sea. Most involved the death of the victim. When Thomas Anstis's crew found a woman among passengers aboard a ship captured off Martinique, 'twenty-one of them forced the poor creature successively', wrote Johnson, 'afterwards broke her back and flung her into the sea'.

Capt. George Lowther and his Company at Port Mayo in the Gulph of Matique.
Engraving after J. Nicholls, nineteenth century.

11
CHAPTER

The Darkest Years of the Golden Age

On 23 November 1718, the day after Blackbeard was killed, Charles Vane spotted what appeared to be a promising prize. But as his brigantine approached what he took to be a harmless merchantman, Vane discovered that his intended prey was nothing less than a French man-of-war. The warship ran out her guns at the same time as she hoisted her colours and, firing a broadside, she prepared to chase the pirates. Most of Vane's men, encouraged by their quartermaster, Jack Rackham, wanted to begin a counter-attack, but Vane refused to directly confront a naval vessel and lost no time in changing course. The following day he lost a vote of confidence and was dumped into a sloop, losing his status, his ship and his reputation.

Although he captured around fifty prizes, Charles Vane never achieved the same notoriety as Edward Thatch. When holding Charleston to ransom Blackbeard had notably commanded a flotilla of vessels. While later preying on ships in the same waters Vane was accompanied by a single vessel commanded by a pirate called Yeats, who felt himself to be so badly treated he went ashore in order to take the king's pardon. Vane never commanded anything as big as the *Queen Anne's Revenge* and his crude brutality lacked Blackbeard's flair for tricks and treachery. After he was deposed, Vane failed to recover his former position and in 1720 he was captured and taken to Jamaica, where he was executed at Gallows Point on 29 March. His hanging body, left 'a sun-drying' in chains on Gun Cay, was a sign of things to come.

The female pirate
Anne Bonny.
Engraving by
F. Wentworth from
Captain Johnson's
A General History of the
Robberies and Murders
of the most Notorious
Pyrates, 1724.

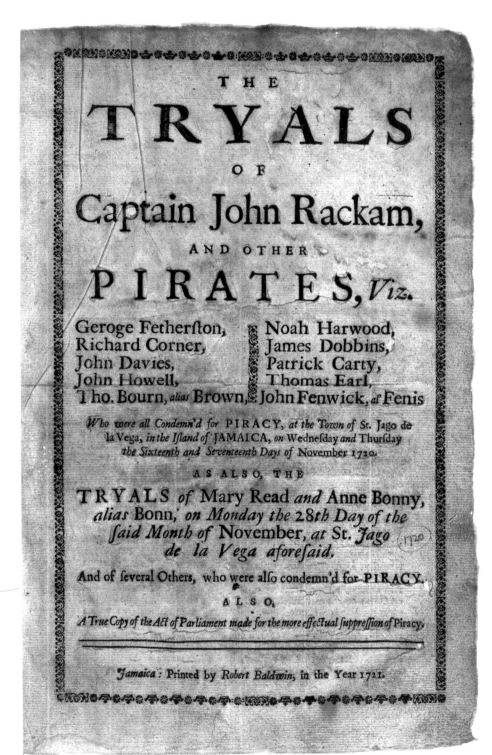

Title page of *The Tryals of Captain John Rackham*, November 1720.

Jack Rackham, whose taste for colourful clothes won him the nickname Calico Jack, went on to plunder small boats across the Caribbean. In May 1719 he arrived at Nassau, where he met Anne Bonny, a girl from Carolina, and persuaded her to run away to sea with him. They subsequently found Mary Read, a well-travelled adventurer and together the three of them lived the life of small-time pirates until discovered off Jamaica by Captain Jonathan Barnet in November 1720. After a brief skirmish in which (according to Captain Johnson) no one fought harder than the two women, Rackham and his crew of eighteen were captured.

Sentenced to death, Rackham was allowed to receive a final visit from Bonny, who comforted her lover with the thought that 'if he had fought like a man, he need not have been hanged like a dog'. Contemporary records show that twelve pirates including Rackham 'were hung on Gibbits in Chains, for a Publick Example, and to terrify others from such-like evil Practices'. Anne Bonny and Mary Read were also condemned to die but each claimed to be 'quick with child'. Physical examinations confirmed they were speaking the truth and both escaped the gallows. In April 1721 Mary Read died of a fever while still in prison; what became of Anne Bonny is not known.

Black Bart Roberts

One result of Woodes Rogers's arrival in Nassau was the dispersal of pirates to regions beyond the West Indies. Men such as Walter Kennedy, Thomas Anstis and Howell Davis – who together captured the sloop *Buck* in New Providence in 1718 – found their way to Africa. It was on Princes Island in the Gulf of Guinea that Davis was eventually killed in 1719.

Davis's crew elected Bartholomew Roberts as their new captain, even though he had been with them for no more than six weeks. 'Black Bart', a tall, dark Welshman, later accomplished one of the boldest raids in pirate history when he plundered a Portuguese treasure ship off the coast of Brazil, stealing 90,000 gold coins and a crucifix set with diamonds that was intended for the king of Portugal. Roberts, who drank tea rather than rum, discouraged gambling and had an interest in religion, managed to capture more than 400 ships in his three-year

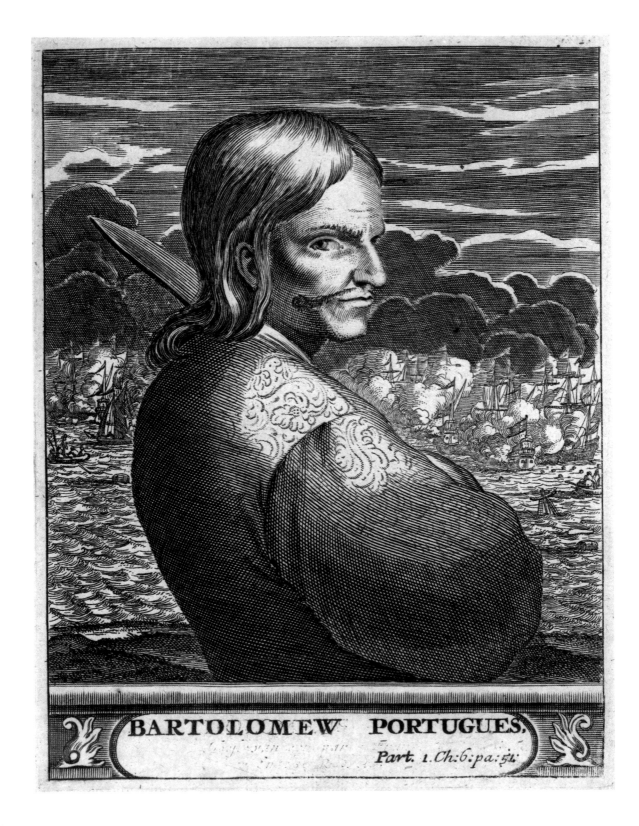

BARTOLOMEW PORTUGUES.

Part. 1. Ch: 6. pa: 51.

'Black Bart' – the notorious Bartholomew Roberts, from a nineteenth-century engraving.

career. He is said to have amassed a fortune that today would be worth around £50 million, and ranks as the most successful captain in the Golden Age of Piracy. A disciplined man with a reputation for ruthlessness, Roberts operated from Newfoundland to Africa's Slave Coast, frequently sailing in consort with other pirates, including Kennedy and Anstis. But for the captains still operating in the early 1720s, time was running out.

By 1718, sea robbers had stoked the wrath of the Establishment in the form of the government, the church and the judiciary. Previously, attempts to deal with the menace of piracy had been restricted to cheaper options such as a general amnesty, rather than expensive alternatives like ships. But the king's pardon, issued in 1717 and extended in 1718, only brought temporary respite, for pardoned pirates often simply did not know what to do with themselves. Many found it hard to resist an 'itching desire to return to their former vile course of life', as Woodes Rogers noted, and dozens, including Blackbeard, went back on the account.

The only solution was to track down individual captains, and kill or capture them – yet not until the death of Blackbeard could the Navy boast of a decisive victory. By 1719 the authorities had finally begun to mobilize their resources in a sustained and co-ordinated campaign to 'cleanse the seas' which was soon supported by additional warships. Over the next few years the nine Navy vessels in the Americas were increased to sixteen, each issued with specific orders to seek out pirates and 'take, burn, sink or otherwise destroy them'. The extra firepower, together with tougher legal measures, led to a growing number of arrests and executions, as pirate captains ran out of places to hide.

In early 1722, Roberts and his 'company of wild ungovernable brutes' found themselves hunted off the west coast of Africa by the 50-gun warship *Swallow*. Commanded by Captain Chaloner Ogle, the *Swallow* had initially been accompanied by another Navy ship, the *Weymouth*, but was forced to go on alone when the latter's crew were laid low by disease. On 10 February, Captain Ogle finally caught up with Roberts off modern-day Gabon.

Admiral Sir Chaloner Ogle,
by a British School artist,
eighteenth century.

Wearing a crimson waistcoat and a hat with a red feather, Roberts armed himself with a brace of pistols and prepared his men for action. Amid 'lightning and thunder and a small tornado', as described by David Cordingly, the *Swallow* fired a devastating broadside, smashing the top of pirates' mizzen-mast and wrecking part of their rigging. In the words of one of the naval officers, the attack was 'immediately returned but without equal damage', and for the next three hours the two ships blazed away at each other.

Many of the pirates were drunk and thus unable to match the naval gunners' ability; they finally lost heart when Roberts was hit in the throat by grapeshot. In accordance with a long-standing wish, he was buried at sea, still in his fine clothes and fully armed. Like Blackbeard's crew before them, the survivors of the battle tried to blow themselves up, defiantly resisting the threat of capture. Approaching the magazine with a lighted match, James Philips was heard 'swearing very prophanely let's all go to hell together'. He was stopped by two men recently captured by the pirates, and in the absence of an explosion his shipmates were captured by the Navy. In April 1722, fifty-two of Roberts's men were hanged outside Cape Coast Castle in modern-day Ghana and another seventeen were jailed in London's Marshalsea Prison. Captain Ogle, who was later made an admiral, received a knighthood for a bold action that marked the beginning of the end of the Golden Age of Piracy.

Brutal recklessness

Marcus Rediker has found that of the 5000 pirates operating between 1716 and 1726, around 500, or one in ten, were hanged. By 1723, a year when eighty-two men were executed, the war against sea robbers raged on both sides of the Atlantic. Battles, disease, imprisonment, accident and suicide also took their toll, so that by 1726 Rediker estimates there were no more than around 200 pirates left. The executions, the bodies left hanging in chains, and the public condemnations by the state, the church and the courts had reduced to a trickle the stream of volunteers on which pirate captains had long relied, so that the surviving commanders had to use 'forced men' more than ever before.

THE MOST NOTORIOUS PIRATES. NO. 4.
PHILIP ROCHE.

[ROCHE AND HIS COMPANIONS DESPATCHING THEIR MASTER AND MATE.]

With increasing numbers of reluctant recruits aboard their ships, only the most ruthless captains could expect to maintain command. Many of them during this period were sadistic even by pirates' standards, and the final and darkest years of the Golden Age were to be marked by a growing tendency towards torture and murder. Captain John Phillips, who had killed his carpenter for 'endeavouring to go off', was himself murdered by Andrew Harradine, a forced man. When John Gow's crew spotted a French merchantman, they were unable to capture her because there were so many men

The 1720s saw a growing tendency towards sadistic acts and murder by pirates at sea, as shown in this engraving of the notorious Philip Roche.

Low presenting a Pistol and Bowl of Punch.

Feared for his cruelty, Edward Low was considered a 'monster' by his own crew. From a nineteenth-century engraving.

aboard who some felt 'they could not confide in'. In frustration, one of the pirates, James Williams, 'proposed to cut all the prisoners throats'.

Men such as Edward Low, who plundered more than 140 vessels in just twenty months, indulged in a brutal recklessness that went beyond the actions of Vane or Blackbeard. Low, whom we last encountered cutting off a man's lips, once thought that the 'greasy' cook of a captured

A pirate about to be hanged at Execution Dock, Wapping. Engraving after Dodd, nineteenth century.

After his hanging at Execution Dock, the body of Captain Kidd was removed to Tilbury Point where it was placed in irons and left to fester for two years as a warning to those tempted by piracy.

vessel would 'fry well', and after tying him to a mast, he set the ship on fire. 'Notorious for his cruelty', one of Low's own men believed that 'a greater monster never infested the seas', and eventually his crew dumped him into an open boat. He was found by the French and hanged at Martinique in 1726.

The execution of Captain John Gow

The fate of Captain John Gow, a Scotsman who turned to piracy following a bloody mutiny, illustrates the treatment that a captured pirate might suffer.

After plundering ships off Portugal he sailed to the Orkneys, where his men killed the mother of two young women who were then 'used in a most inhumane manner'. Arrested in February 1725, he was brought to London and thrown into the Marshalsea prison. Gow refused to plead, and in an attempt to force him to do so, his thumbs were tied together by the executioner and an assistant, 'they drawing the cord till it broke'. He still refused and was sentenced to be pressed: a slow, agonizing torture which involved heavy stones being placed on the victim's body, sometimes for days at a time. He eventually declared his innocence, allowing the trial to begin.

On 26 May, Gow was convicted of piracy, along with eight of his men, and three weeks later he was taken in a cart from the Marshalsea over London Bridge and past the Tower of London, to Wapping. Travelling in a procession led by the Admiralty marshal carrying a silver oar, Gow was attended by the prison chaplain as he was taken to the gallows that were set up near the low-tide mark at Execution Dock. Here pirates had been hanged since medieval times, among them Captain William Kidd in 1701. Gow was pushed off a ladder by the executioner, and as he slowly strangled, his friends pulled his legs to quicken his death. Their forceful efforts snapped the rope and Gow had to be strung up for a second time. After his death, three tides were allowed to pass over his body before his remains were weather-proofed with tar and suspended beside the Thames in a gibbet (an iron cage), where they served as a grim warning to all who might be tempted to take up piracy.

Defiant to the last

Executions, like trials, were accompanied by lengthy readings from the Bible as priests urged the condemned to make their peace with God. Some pirates sought salvation through confession. John Rose Archer, condemned in Boston in 1724, regretted that he'd 'provoked the Holy One ... to leave me unto the Crimes of Pyracy'. For those confronted by zealous preachers like Cotton Mather, finding one's peace was not always easy. In 1717, Mather's frenzied hand-wringing tone eventually whipped John Brown into a state of mania that stranded him somewhere between repentance and confusion. 'I know not where to begin,' muttered Brown, 'I may begin with gaming! No, whoring, that led on to gaming; and gaming led on to drinking; and drinking to lying, and swearing and cursing, and all that is bad; and so to thieving; and to this!'

Many, however, died as they lived: in defiance. There was nowhere better to demonstrate their bravado than at the gallows, which came equipped with a ready-made audience that held its breath while waiting for a man's last words. 'I am extremely sorry,' said one pirate after being urged to repent, 'that you ain't all hanged as well'. Thomas Morris, condemned in the Bahamas in 1718, wished he'd been a 'greater Plague to these Islands'. After arriving at the scaffold in Boston in 1726, William Fly lectured the hangman 'for not understanding his Trade' and offered to teach him how to tie a proper noose.

The ruthlessness of the war against pirates influenced the behaviour of men like Phillips, Gow and Low. Ultimately their acts of violence reached the point where the spirit of easygoing freedom, enjoyed by the likes of Blackbeard, was long forgotten and men stopped volunteering to go on the account. The tide had turned once the Navy started to hit back; in the war with the authorities, pirates were forced to think not of freedom but of survival. Compared to the capture of Roberts's crew, the Battle of Ocracoke may have been small – but it was a key moment in the long history of robbery at sea.

Anne Bonny and Mary Read

The stories of Anne Bonny and Mary Read, the only two female pirates known to have existed in the West Indies, almost defy belief. Born around 1680, Mary Read was supposedly brought up as a boy in a deception designed to win money from her relatives. As a teenager she maintained the disguise and joined a cavalry regiment in Flanders, where she fell in love with a Flemish soldier. They married and bought an inn, but around 1697 Mary's husband died. Joining a vessel bound for the West Indies, she was captured by pirates, who eventually took her to the Bahamas. There she adopted their way of life.

Born around 1685, Anne Bonny was said to be the illegitimate child of an Irish lawyer and a maidservant, whose relationship caused such a scandal that they eventually took Anne to seek a new life in the Carolinas. Anne, too, was brought up as a boy, and grew into a strong woman, possessing 'a fierce and courageous temper'. Disowned by her father after marrying a local boy, she moved to Nassau before running away to sea with the pirate captain Jack Rackham.

MARY READ, A FEMALE PIRATE.

MARY READ KILLING ONE OF HER OWN CREW, IN SINGLE COMBAT.

In action, Anne wore men's clothes and helped to keep the cannon supplied with powder. Following one skirmish, while still in her disguise, she took a liking to a new recruit; but when she revealed her true sex to the man, she discovered to her astonishment that 'he', too, was a woman – Mary Read.

Rackham's crew openly accepted the presence of Anne and Mary – probably because the two women shared everything that a pirate's life involved, including both the rewards and the dangers – and Mary Read soon found herself a lover among the men. Discovering this man had been challenged to a duel, and fearing for his ability to defend himself, Mary boldly picked an argument with the challenger herself and arranged to fight him two hours before her partner. She killed the man on the spot.

Anne and Mary stayed aboard Rackham's boat until the end, both gaining a reputation for ability and bravery. There is every possibility that women secretly worked on other pirate ships, but their names were never recorded. At least one example of the pirate code made it an offence to bring a woman aboard a ship, since seamen's jealousies could easily erupt into violence; to protect themselves from harm, women may have hidden their identities, as Mary Read tried to do.

MARIE READ.

Right: Mary Read revealing her sex, after Alexandre Debelle, from P. Christian's *Histoire des Pirates*, 1852.

Left: Mary Read killing one of her own crew, in single combat. From a nineteenth-century engraving.

Pirates in Film and Fiction

The rich mix of pirate folklore and legend has inspired poems, books and films, from Byron's *The Corsair* to J. M. Barrie's *Peter Pan* and Disney's *Pirates of the Caribbean*. Combining tales from the buccaneers, Captain Johnson and the Cuban pirates, writers and directors have created a hotchpotch of fact and fiction spiced up with Latin lovers, chests of buried treasure, and the mandatory talking parrot. Robert Louis Stevenson's *Treasure Island*, which single-handedly invented the concept of the treasure map, was initially published in instalments, beginning in 1881. Through characters drawn partly from Johnson, such as the one-legged sea cook Long John Silver, Israel Hands (who served with Blackbeard) and the rough old tar Billy Bones, the novel swings from adventure and comradeship to violence and treachery in a successful attempt to pin down the spirit of piracy.

The following text labels appear on the costume design:

Tarnished Gold Lace

Wig should be made of Black Chenille or Blacket possible stuff. so as to catch no light whatever

Hair Curls uncurled

Soiled Shirt

Brown leather patches to hold 3 pistols each side in soft braces

Coat to be a dusty Blue Black with pale Blue lining

Pistols to be at this angle:—

Soiled Lace

Pistol Very Sharp

Sash to be colour of dry Blood:—

Pocket

Rusty Buckles

To Audry from

Captain Hook—

Above: Costume design for Captain Hook from J. M. Barrie's *Peter Pan*.

Left: The Pirates of Cuba, from a nineteenth-century engraving.

At least five films have been based on the story of *Treasure Island*, including Disney's 1950 version starring Robert Newton as Silver. Two years later Newton played the lead in *Blackbeard the Pirate*, in which Maynard finds himself working undercover aboard the pirate ship until distracted by the charms of Edwina Mansfield (Linda Darnell), whom Blackbeard has kidnapped. In these films Newton muttered a few pirate 'aaarrs' in his native West Country accent, setting the tone for pirate voices ever since. *The Curse of the Black Pearl* (2003), the first film in Disney's *Pirates of the Caribbean* trilogy, is a sweeping adventure story featuring Johnny Depp as Captain Jack Sparrow, a completely reckless and slightly intoxicated pirate captain. Sparrow must take on the ghostly crew of the *Black Pearl* if he is to save the gorgeous Elizabeth Swann (Keira Knightley) from the clutches of the cursed Captain Barbossa. Needless to say, Sparrow is fictional, but Depp adopts a dishevelled, carefree manner that is far closer to the real thing than the polished, swashbuckling heroes of earlier pirate epics, such as Errol Flynn in *The Sea Hawk*. Indeed, Sparrow bears more than a passing resemblance to the real pirate Jack Rackham.

Right: From stage to screen to concert hall, the popularized image was often one of dashing, daring or jolly rogues. *The Pirates of Penzance* – cover for a quadrille dance by Charles d'Albert, published by Chappell & Co., late nineteenth century.

Left: Robert Newton in the title role of *Blackbeard the Pirate* (film by Raoul Welsh, 1952).

Sunken Treasures

Piercing the shallow waters of Beaufort Inlet, shafts of light glittered on the silver bodies of inquisitive fish. Before reaching the seabed, 22 ft down, the sunrays dissolved into an emerald gloom giving just enough light for two divers to spot what they had been looking for. A small reef, teeming with sea-life, was strewn with cannon, anchors and ballast stones from a ship long believed to have been swallowed up by the shifting sands of the ocean floor. Over many subsequent dives archaeologists have since recovered scientific instruments, wine bottles still intact and guns still loaded, and while the case has not been proved conclusively, few seriously doubt that after nearly 300 years Blackbeard's flagship has been found.

Discovered on 21 November 1996 by the shipwreck exploration firm Intersal, the wreck is all that remains of a 90-ft, well-armed, eighteenth-century vessel. She had heeled over on her port side, spilling cannon and cargo into the sea a mile south of the island of Bogue Banks, North Carolina. So far, more than 15,000 artefacts have been recovered, and most have been transferred to the North Carolina Maritime Museum. They are essential clues in one of the most intriguing mysteries in maritime archaeology. The search for an answer as to whether this really is the *Queen Anne's Revenge* is being managed by dozens of experts from the Maritime Museum, the Underwater Archaeology Branch of the North Carolina state government, and other institutions who, together, participate in the *Queen Anne's Revenge* Shipwreck Project.

The artefacts can be divided into two groups: those directly associated with the structure or operation of the ship and those that

The *Queen Anne's Revenge* Shipwreck Project, 1998: the retrieval of a cannon (cannon C4).

once belonged to an individual. Little is left of the vessel itself, but oak planks recovered from the hull have been radiocarbon-dated by the Woods Hole Oceanographic Institution in Massachusetts. Their results suggest the ship was built between 1690 and 1710. Her ballast stones are largely of Caribbean basalt but also include limestone indigenous to France and West Africa, supporting the idea that she was a French vessel involved in the slave trade. Other items include anchors, barrel hoops, rings relating to the rigging and a grappling hook. There are iron nails that could have been used either in repairs or as ammunition, while decorative lead tacks, discovered towards the stern of the ship, may have been used in furniture. A bronze bell, recovered on the day the wreck was found, is of Spanish origin and bears the date 1705.

The Shipwreck Project has so far identified twenty-four cannon, eight of which have been lifted from the seabed. They include two retrieved in the summer of 2005 (one weighing 2400 lbs), as well as two 6-pounder guns (*i.e.* they fired a six-pound ball), each weighing nearly 2000 lbs and possibly of French origin. A three-pounder and a half-

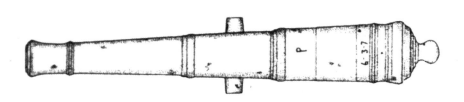

Line drawing of Cannon C4, retrieved by the Shipwreck Project.

pounder, both British, and a slightly larger Swedish gun, dated 1713, have also been found. So, too, has an object covered with concreted ballast stones, which appears to be a small-calibre cannon.

The fact that these guns are of various sizes and, according to the Shipwreck Project, originate from at least two and probably three different countries, suggests that they were assembled in a ramshackle way. This is not something a merchant captain would be likely to do, much less the Royal Navy, but is just the sort of thing that might be expected of pirates. The thirty-eight cannon-balls recovered so far include bar-shot, designed to disable ships, and twenty-four-pound shot, suggesting the vessel carried relatively large guns. Four of the cannon were loaded, one with three large spikes intended to kill people rather than damage a vessel. This resembles the tactic used at Ocracoke when lethal partridge-shot claimed many casualties in the broadside that opened the battle. Maynard's men also encountered hand grenades, and similar examples were found on the wreck in 1998.

Restoring a name

In looking for direct evidence of the ship's captain and his men, personal objects of everyday use reveal much about the crew. These were men who liked to drink. Three intact onion-shaped wine bottles have been found, all made of green glass and following a pattern fashionable around 1710. In the spring of 2005, divers recovered a valuable piece of evidence when they spotted the stem of a wineglass embossed with small diamonds and crowns, made to commemorate the coronation of King George I in 1714.

No blades have been found, but the brass barrel of an English blunderbuss (dating from between 1672 and 1702) has been retrieved, as have many musket balls and lead shot of various sizes. A lead sounding-weight and parts of scientific instruments used for navigation have also been identified. Other personal items include platters, plates

A urethral syringe (length 6.3 in.) with curved funnel tip. Retrieved by the *Queen Anne's Revenge* Shipwreck Project.

and a dish (all made of pewter), a clay pipe, a beer bottle and pieces of a jar similar to those once used in Virginia to store liquids such as oil. A fearsome urethral syringe, over six inches long, has a curved funnel tip and was used to administer mercury for the treatment of sexually transmitted diseases. The strongest clue so far that this is a wreck associated with pirates lies in the discovery of seventy flakes of gold dust, which together weigh 0.07oz.

As well as examining artefacts found on the wreck, it is important to look at where it lies. The ship sank while approaching Beaufort Inlet, known in the eighteenth century as Topsail Inlet, a narrow channel between the islands of Bogue Banks and Shackleford Banks. On the mainland, less than two miles away, lies the town of Beaufort which, according to Johnson, was formerly 'a poor little village at the upper end of the harbour'.

In Blackbeard's day, Beaufort had few links with the interior of

Gold dust (intermixed with lead shot and sand), retrieved from the south end of the site by the *Queen Anne's Revenge* Shipwreck Project.

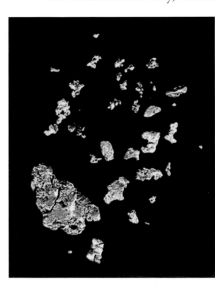

the country and did not trade with any ship larger than a small coastal vessel. Indeed, the only significant port anywhere in the Carolinas was Charleston. Converse Clowse found that in 1718 the average size of the ten biggest vessels leaving Charleston was 107 tons. In 1724, the first full year covered by local data on armaments, larger ships using the port carried an average of five guns and few vessels were stronger than the 20-gun Carolina station ship *Flamborough*. The vessel wrecked in Beaufort Inlet was carrying at least twenty-four cannon, and such a large and powerful ship would have stood out even in a busy port like Charleston. Her presence close to a remote fishing village with no significant commerce is, in the words of the historian Lindley Butler, 'not only an anomaly but is in fact extraordinary'.

Over the centuries scores of vessels have been lost after straying too close to Beaufort's stretch of the coast. The Shipwreck Project has noted that of the historically documented wrecks in the general Cape Lookout area, only two occurred between 1709 and 1724 in the area surrounding the inlet: the *Queen Anne's Revenge* and the *Adventure*.

In June 1718, witnesses such as David Herriot saw the *Queen Anne's Revenge* 'run a-ground off of the Bar of Topsail-Inlet', and the governor of Bermuda believed that at the time the ship was carrying thirty-six guns. The director of the Shipwreck Project has been quoted as saying that so far less than five per cent of the site has been excavated. It may be that in the not-too-distant future conclusive evidence will be found, and the wreck that is currently listed as 31CR314 will once again officially become the *Queen Anne's Revenge*.

'A roaring, swaggering, swearing pirate'

Inspired by the likes of Drake and Morgan, seamen in the early eighteenth century became adept at capturing vessels while serving aboard privateers during the War of the Spanish Succession. When peace came in 1713, the hunt for French and Spanish loot officially ended, and so did sailors' hopes of legitimate wealth. Seamen's jobs began to dry up and any work still available aboard slave-ships or merchant vessels offered low pay and grim conditions.

Only money bought freedom from service aboard such ships. For a seaman skilled in plundering vessels there was a great temptation to ignore the peace treaty and carry on as before. Men such as Hornigold and Jennings chose to do as the merchants did and make easy money from ships, specifically those that were French or Spanish. Such bold thinking renewed sailors' hopes of riches and freedom and rekindled the excitement they had discovered during the war. But once they had made some cash, Hornigold and Jennings retired to enjoy it at the first opportunity, taking the king's pardon in early 1718. Like them, many pirate captains operating in 1716 and 1717 were only in it for the money. They were reluctant to attack

Next page: 'A ranting, roaring, swaggering, swearing pirate': Blackbeard and his crew (Still from the television film).

English ships, they were not particularly violent, and when given a way out they quickly took it, peacefully working with the authorities in the form of colonial governors.

But they had set into motion something that developed into far more than they imagined. Other, younger, captains were not interested in retirement. From the outset pirates at this time were eminently successful, and for the lucky few, vast amounts of treasure were there for the taking, as Sam Bellamy proved. These men routinely preyed on an apparently endless supply of vulnerable merchant ships and eventually became hooked to things that shone more brightly than gold. Their initial spirit of adventure evolved into defiance and a sense of power, and together these things took pirates a step beyond the likes of Hornigold. Men abandoned any lingering loyalty to the country they came from and stood united in freedom, sharing a common code and declaring war on the world. For them it was not just about the cash it was about the life itself.

Bellamy, Vane, Rackham, Roberts and Low all made money at one stage or another, though none of them could bring themselves to enjoy it properly, preferring instead a life at sea. In turning their back on the authorities they chose a lifestyle that was certainly merry but inevitably short. Only Blackbeard succeeded in having it all – nearly. Sometime between the siege of Charleston and arriving at Topsail Inlet he saw that his old master, Hornigold, had been right. Clutching his wealth (and other people's, too), Edward Thatch arranged a pardon for himself, along with a home and a wife, and tried to settle down. But it was too late. Having tasted the freedom that existed beyond the routine of civilized life, he found it too hard to give up, and carried on with piracy. His downfall lay in the fact that he preyed on ships in an area where the authorities were ready to fight back. Yet his reputation lives on: more than 150 years after his death, a North Carolina newspaper wrote that 'Blackbeard will ever remain a ranting, roaring, swaggering, swearing pirate'.

Let's hope they're right.

Piracy after Blackbeard

The extra warships sent to the colonial stations by the Admiralty in the 1720s and after, successfully prevented further periods of piracy for almost 100 years. Here and there reports emerged of vessels plundered at sea, but not with the same frequency as in the past. Other maritime powers experienced greater difficulties in tackling the problem. Napoléon's conquest of Spain in 1808 severed the country's links with her Caribbean interests, triggering the Latin American wars of independence that brought a corresponding rise in piracy. This reached a climax in the early 1820s.

Cuban pirates of this period were noted for a general level of brutality that went beyond even the lip-slicing atrocities of Edward Low. A report sent to the Secretary of the United States in 1823 described these men as the 'most bloodthirsty monsters that ever disgraced the name of man'. In his book *The Pirate Wars*, Peter Earle reveals stories of victims nailed to the deck or roasted on slow fires. Another form of execution, recorded by *The Times* in 1822 and in 1829, involved walking the plank – which has since popularly, though mistakenly, come to be attributed to all pirates. After committing an array of excesses on the high seas, these swarthy and moustachioed men (as they are described by contemporary newspaper articles), apparently merrily returned to their guitars and *señoritas*.

Today pirates continue to haunt many parts of the world, particularly South-East Asia, West Africa and the north-east coast of South America. One attack that took place in the waters off Peru involved 'robbers armed with long knives boarding a ship at [the] forecastle'. The thieves stole the vessel's stores before escaping in a fishing boat, in a raid that dates not from the eighteenth century but from August 2005.

In 1992, The International Maritime Bureau set up the Piracy Reporting Centre following an alarming rise in robberies. In 2004 the centre was informed of about 325 attacks worldwide, compared to 445 the previous year. Although 2004 saw a fall in actual raids, the number of murders rose from twenty-one to thirty.

We tend to think of today's pirates as somehow different from Blackbeard and his contemporaries, who in the 300 years since their time have taken on a romantic appearance. To us they have become swashbuckling rogues, while modern thieves are sometimes seen as sinister men, more akin to terrorists than pirates. One website that discusses the work of the International Maritime Bureau says that 'piracy still exists in the modern world, but it has reached new heights and is seemingly out of control'. This suggests the atrocities of modern-day pirates are more appalling than those committed in the past and are only likely to get worse. Yet the author of a letter sent from Jamaica to the Council of Trade and Plantations in 1716 said exactly the same thing: '... the evil encreases ... I can see no full and effectual end of these things'.

Blackbeard, the Television Film

This book accompanies a multimillion-pound film for television – *Blackbeard: The Real Pirate of the Caribbean* – that re-creates the final years of Blackbeard's life. Starring James Purefoy and directed by Richard Dale and Tilman Remme, the production, made by Dangerous Films, was largely shot over two months on a huge water-tank beside the sea in Malta. This offered the producers a controlled environment with uninterrupted views reaching out to the horizon beneath Caribbean-style sunshine.

More than forty craftsmen spent two months building a full-size sloop (serving as the *Revenge*, the *Adventure* and the *Jane*), which was rigged by experts who normally work on the *Cutty Sark*, Greenwich, and other historic ships. The team also built and rigged part of a second sloop and the (almost full-size) stern of the *Queen Anne's Revenge*. The vessels were armed with twenty cannon, each equipped with tackle and tools, and six of these guns were able to make realistic 'live-fire' explosions. Two fully rigged models of a sloop and a ship, each around twenty feet long, were used in wide shots.

The cast, trained to fight by stuntmen, were issued with more than 150 muskets and cutlasses along with a further forty rubber copies. In two months the flintlock pistols fired more gunpowder than would have been used by real pirates over the same period of time. After they had completed their raiding and plundering, the cast returned to the UK to shoot the Spotswood and Eden scenes. The film crew produced a total of seventy hours of footage, shooting about six minutes of television a day.

Above: Behind the scenes in the making of the film: James Purefoy in the title role.

Next page: The crew of the film on location in Malta.

Sources and Further Reading

Evelyn Berckman, *Victims of Piracy* (London, 1979)

Clinton V. Black, *Pirates of the West Indies* (Cambridge, 1989)

Jean Boudriot, *The History of the French Frigate 1650 – 1850* (Heathfield, 1993)

H. H. Chapelle, *The Search for Speed under Sail* (London, 1983)

David Cordingly, *Life Among the Pirates* (London, 1995)

David Cordingly and John Falconer, *Pirates Facts and Fiction* (London, 1992)

G.F. Dow. & J.H. Edmonds, *The Pirates of the New England Coast* (Salem, 1923)

Alexandre-Olivier Exquemelin, *Exquemelin and the Pirates of the Caribbean* (Oxford, 1993)

John Harland, *Seamanship in the Age of Sail* (London, 1984)

Marshall Delancey Haywood, *Governor Charles Eden* (Raleigh, 1903)

Captain Charles Johnson *A General History of the Robberies and Murders of the Most Notorious Pirates* (London, 1724, and London, 1998)

Bjorn Landstrom, *The Ship* (London, 1961)

Kris Lane, *Blood and Silver: Piracy in the Americas, 1500-1750* (Oxford, 1999)

Brian Lavery, *The Arming and Fitting of English Ships of War 1600 – 1815* (London, 1987)

Brian Lavery, *Nelson's Navy: The Ships, Men and Organization, 1793-1815* (Annapolis, 2003)

Brian Lavery, *The Ship of the Line: Design, Construction and Fittings Vols 1 & 2* (London, 2004

Robert E. Lee, *Blackbeard the Pirate: A Reappraisal of His Life and Times* (Winston-Salem, 1974)

David Marley, *Pirates and Privateers of the Americas* (Santa Barbara, 1994)

Patrick Pringle, *The Jolly Roger: The Story of the Great Age of Piracy* (London, 1953)

Marcus Rediker, *Between the Devil and the Deep Blue Sea* (Cambridge, 1987)

Marcus Rediker, *Villains of All Nations* (London, 2004)

Aaron Smith, *The Atrocities of Pirates* (London, 1997)

Judge Nicholas Trott, *Tryals of Stede Bonnet and Other Pirates* (London, 1719)

Julie Wheelright, *Amazons and Military Maids* (London, 1989)

S Wilkinson, *The Voyages and Adventures of Edward Teach* (Boston, 1808)

George Woodbury, *The Great Days of Piracy in the West Indies* (New York, 1951)

The Archives Départementales Loire-Atlantique contain much information with regard to *La Concorde*, (which later became the *Queen Anne's Revenge*), including descriptions of the loss of the ship to Blackbeard, written by Captain Pierre Dosset and Lieutenant François Ernaut.

The National Archives in London also hold much of value including letters left by Governor Spotswood, and Captain Ellis Brand, as well as the *Calendar of State Papers, Colonial Series, America and West Indies*.

The National Maritime Museum in London holds the log of the *Pearl*, including Maynard's journal detailing his departure from the ship in November 1718, and his return with Blackbeard's head in January 1719.

Picture Acknowledgements

National Maritime Museum
Images from the collection of the National Maritime Museum are listed below with their page and reproduction numbers. They may be ordered by writing to the Picture Library, National Maritime Museum, Greenwich, SE10 9NF, United Kingdom, or online at www.nmm.ac.uk/picturelibrary, tel. 00 44 (0)20 8312 6631. All images copyright © National Maritime Museum, London

Pages: **2** PW2577; **3** D3864-21 (detail); **20** A1607; **22–23** BHC0849; **24** PU5126; **26** PU2637; **29** D8908-1 (left); **29** D8821-2 (right) **29** F2522 (below); **31** D7491-2; **32** D7531-1; **33** F0252; **35** PW4966; **37** D7531–11; **42–3** BHC1841; **46–7** F1796; **48–9** BHC0747; **50** D7529-6; **53** D6169-1; **60–1** ZBA2429 (Michael Graham-Stewart Slavery Collection. Acquired with the assistance of the Heritage Lottery Fund); **64** D7531-10; **66** 3633; **76–7** BHC2973; **78–9** D7767; **81** E3089-1;2; **83** D3829; **95** D6170-1; **97** PU8484; **100–1** D7531-3; **106** F4083; **108–9** PX9753; **115** D7491-4; **118** D6870 (top); **119** PW5940; **137** D3864-21; **138** D6096; **139** E8768 (top); **139** E1410 (bottom); **155** D7491-6; **157** 7751; **160** D7529-2; **162** BHC2917; **164** D7501; **165** D7491-5; **166** 6588; **167** D3864-15; **168** D7504-3; **169** D6170-3; **172** D7504-8; **173** D7520; **174** D7519

Illustrations are also reproduced by kind permission of the following:

Dangerous Films Ltd 2005/Kurt Arrigo – *pages:* **11**; **17**; **19**; **55**; **69**; **73**; **94**; **111**; **117**; **123**; **124–25**; **131**; **132–33**; **135**; **144–45**; **182–83**; **187**; **188–89**
Dangerous Films Ltd 2005/ Nion Hazell – *pages* **2**; **3** and ship backgrounds throughout

Bridgeman Art Library/Bristol City Art Gallery) – *page* **15**
Bridgeman Art Library/The British Library – *page* **41**
Bridgeman Art Library/Library of Congress, Washington D.C) – *page* **143**
Bridgeman Art Library/© Ferens Art Gallery, Hull City Museums and Art Galleries – *page* **86–7**
Guildhall Library, Corporation of London – *pages* **140–41**
Image Library, National Archives, Kew (CO 137/14 folio 9) – *page* **158**
Kobal Collection, London – *page* **180**
© Library of Virginia – *page* **104**
Queen Anne's Revenge Shipwreck Project. Courtesy North Carolina Department of Cultural Resources – *pages* **177**; **178**; **179**

Map artwork – *pages:* **6–7**; **93** Jamie Crocker, artista-design.co.uk
Cover artwork – Gary Alake Riley & Marcus Freeman © BBC Worldwide

Blackbeard: The Real Pirate of the Caribbean

First published in North America by
Thunder's Mouth Press,
by arrangement with
National Maritime Museum Publishing, London, 2006

Thunder's Mouth Press
An imprint of Avalon Publishing Group, Inc.
245 West 17th St., 11th floor
New York, NY 10011

AVALON
publishing group incorporated

Library of Congress Cataloging-in-Publication Data is available.

ISBN 1-56025-885-3
ISBN-13 978-1-56025-885-8

9 8 7 6 5 4 3 2 1

Cover artwork by Gary Alake Riley and Marcus Freeman © BBC Worldwide
Book design by Mousemat Design Ltd
Printed and bound in the UK by Butler and Tanner